Dog Bless You

Discovering God's Love Through Man's Best Friend

Alex Miller

Made for Success Publishing
www.MadeForSuccess.com

Distributed by Blackstone Publishing

First Printing
Library of Congress Cataloging-in-Publication data
Miller, Alex
    Dog Bless You:
    p. cm.

LCCN: 2025936349
ISBN: 978-1-64146-934-0 *(pbk)*
ISBN: 978-1-64146-935-7 *(eBook)*
ISBN: 978-1-64146-936-4 *(audio)*

Printed in the United States of America

For further information, contact Made for Success Publishing
+1 (425) 526-6480 or email service@madeforsuccess.net.

To my daughters: If kindness were a person and love was a picture, there you would be—together.

TABLE OF CONTENTS

STORY COMPANIONS

Zeus

Max

Ben

INTRODUCTION

This isn't a dog book. But don't panic.

I know right now you're thinking, "Wait, what?" So, let me explain.

This is a "thank goodness for grace, kitchen table full of love" kind of book. It's a personal account of growing closer to truth, faith, redemption, and a life of understanding. It showcases the pure serenity of seeing God's presence in the things we love and the struggle we often endure in allowing Him to bless us.

I believe God presents Himself in many of the ordinary, everyday things we love, but sometimes, we're too busy to truly see Him. For instance, if my husband, Devon, were to show me a diagram of the new Corvette engine (although I'll admit it's impressive), I probably wouldn't see Him. However, it never fails when a dog runs up to me. I smile and say, "Thanks, God. I needed that."

We all have that unexplainable thing that just lures us in. When Devon sees a fast car, he always exclaims, "Jiminy Christmas!" Obviously, fast, sleek cars and boats are his love language with God. The best part is that it doesn't matter that my love language is completely different from his. I just feel incredibly blessed that both our hearts house "lures" that make us better versions of ourselves. God isn't trying to change us, just simply trying to engage us.

Okay, now get ready to really say, "Wait, what?"

I can't believe I'm about to admit this, but I used to be a cat person. Hopefully, the rest of this book will redeem me from that statement. Not that there's anything wrong with cats at all! But I was the silly little girl in her oversized cat sweater, counting and rearranging her feline figurines in every spare moment. It's okay to laugh—it sounds as weird as it was.

To be honest, I don't even know where my love (borderline obsession) really came from. I only had cats growing up, so I assume it started there. I loved what I knew and was comfortable with the idea of cute, cuddly kittens. If you think about it, it's a merry-go-round that I think many of us hop right on. Familiarity breeds comfort, and cats were my happy place.

But then it happened. I woke up one day allergic to cats. Yep, I'm serious, just out of the blue. And not just some cats—all cats. My cat, the neighbor's cat, and even the stray cat I thought I could pick up if I used a towel instead of my hands. It was devastating, but looking back, I realize God was preparing me for a much bigger, less itchy, over-the-top kind of love. We've all heard that God prepares us for our passions and desires. Sometimes, it's puzzling to grasp that we may not yet be ready for what we truly need, and the prep work takes time. For me, it was a couple of swollen eyes, a rash, and an empty Kleenex box. But it was all totally worth it!

So, with my cat-cuddling days behind me, it was time for a new plan. My family found my cat a new home, and all my beloved kitty knick-knacks were boxed up. As I grew up, my cat collection faded further into a distant memory with each passing day. Don't get me wrong—I will always have a special place in my heart for our furry feline friends. Occasionally, I will see a kitten or a tomcat begging for attention or a scrumptious little snack, and while I have no desire to scoop them up and snuggle them, my adult self acknowledges their presence with delight in some unconscious attempt to foster the child within. I love the moment you realize "adult you" is precisely the person "child you" needed.

Throughout college, the box of kitty-cat collectibles traveled from place to place with me. I'll admit, back then, I had a problem with placing sentimental value on too many things. Eventually, my once-beloved collection found itself in a house fire, and only one cat ornament survived. Untouched in storage for years, this was probably best, as college often finds people in the smallest apartments, and the box was not exactly anyone's favorite centerpiece.

Luckily, I didn't mourn this material loss much, as I had just gotten my first puppy, Max (you'll meet him in a bit), and we were moving into our first house. Little did I know that God was about to introduce me to the next "forever lure" of my life. The lone porcelain cat ornament came with us and was stuck in the attic for safekeeping, along with a stash of other "assets." The crazy thing about attic storage items is you only need them once the ladder goes up. So, in the process of moving things around to find something I can't even remember now, that solitary cat came crashing down onto the concrete floor.

But lo and behold—and I kid you not—that darned cat did not break!

Fire-stained and with a small chip on its ear, that cat still sits in my closet today. It's a heartfelt reminder of who I am and where I've been. Something doesn't have to consume you to be a part of you. The feline figurine's subtle way of showing up in my life over and over has been one of the loudest voices I've heard over the years. From time to time, my foundation has been covered in soot, and most of my walls have cracks and chips, but I appreciate every imperfection because it has brought me home. The twists and turns have brought me to my relationship with Jesus through dogs and in any other way He chooses to illustrate His love in my crazy daily life.

Dogs are the "lure" that attaches my soul to something so much purer than myself. If my legacy doesn't involve the term "crazy dog lady," then I probably didn't fully take advantage of my purpose. And that is how this book was born!

I haven't always felt God's presence, but that has more to do with me than Him. Sometimes, I overthink and overanalyze. Would I know Him in the moment? Would He tap me on the shoulder? I imagine Him passing me in traffic, waving happily with the windows rolled down in a Jeep full of Labradors. Ridiculous, I know, and I'd bet most of my life savings that it doesn't quite work that way. But it's fun to imagine.

Most importantly, I feel that whenever I've needed Him, He's been there, and most of the time, it's been in the form of a good old pooch!

As children, we hide our eyes under a blanket from monsters, shadows, and the dark. We find relief in believing, "If I can't see them, they can't see me." This blanket fort, where the unknown, scary darkness doesn't exist, gives us the comfort of being in control. But if we aren't careful, I think we often find ourselves creating blanket forts that withstand more than intended.

This is where I raise my hand and admit, "This is me." I'm definitely guilty of living what I like to call a "syllabus life." What's that, you ask? Remember those dreaded course syllabi teachers used to pass out in high school and college? Well, a syllabus life is one where you can mark milestones and expectations off a list and hide behind the satisfaction of knowing you have prepared perfectly for what's to come. It sounds organized and pristine, but really, it's just plain unrealistic.

Life is a messy, beautiful dance (with dogs, in my case).

Perhaps this is why it is difficult for me to understand the phrase "trying to find God." Once I stopped hiding in my blanket fort, He was right there waiting for me. You should have seen all the puppies and dog hair that flooded into my life!

I'll be perfectly straight with you: in life, you have to find your keys, your jacket, and often, your wallet. But God—never. Think about it. Do you really need to find someone who is with you all the time? Someone who never leaves your side? If you poke your head out from under your covers for a split second, you'll be amazed at your view: furry canines, fast cars, a mountain hike, or a red bird. I don't know what yours will be, but I know it'll be breathtaking.

So, find your lure.

Embrace God's blessings.

Let your journey truly begin.

Chapter 1

MEET MAX

I need . . .

Sometimes, we know we need something, but we're not sure what that "something" is.

Looking back, I realize many moments in my childhood were filled with self-doubt and constant questioning of my worth. Like many of us, I masked my uncertainty with perfect grades and worked over-the-top hard at everything I did. I was on this soul-searching mission that I now recognize as my personal quest for the love of Jesus.

Something inside me just knew there was something more. Moving into my teens, I started recognizing that the people who loved me in the most meaningful ways were the ones who loved Christ the most. Even knowing this, it still took me years to commit my life to Him. I could not understand how just being me was enough to be a child of God. There were no other requirements. But that's hard to fathom sometimes, isn't it?

I like to believe He knew I needed a little piece of heaven on Earth—and that's exactly what He sent. He knew I needed Max so I could finally understand my value through God's eyes. Meeting Max was the moment I found my love language with God. This was the moment I found the goodness that would stay with me for the rest of my life—the goodness in me. I finally realized I am a beautiful child of God, and that is good enough.

As always, God's timing is beautiful, and I marvel at the idea that He sent a two-pound Pomeranian to illustrate the love of the world—or at least my world. That is what great teachers do. They see where their students are and lovingly meet them there. I had never had a puppy in my life, and as I said in the introduction to this book, I wasn't even sure if dogs were "my thing."

But I like to jump into things with both feet, so I started talking about the possibility of owning a dog and making lists of what it would entail. A dog would definitely be a financial responsibility, and it would need ample space and attention. But at the time, my husband, Devon, and I were financially struggling college students living in a small apartment with obligations on campus and jobs.

Since I had a lot to juggle, I understood I was on the low end of the "Most Qualified Dog Mom" list. So, Devon offered me a deal. He said, "If you can pretend to have a pet for a week and keep it alive, we can get a dog."

Ummm, challenge accepted—as crazy as that sounds. It's important to note that I'm still this stubborn. So, off I went on my fake dog journey. I walked, "watered," and loved that precious little air dog. At the end of the week, Devon admitted he'd really thought the deal would get him out of the situation. I mean, who would take care of a pretend dog anyway?

The answer is me! And my life was about to change.

We started looking for the perfect pup, and we found Max. It wasn't that he was physically perfect (although I didn't know that yet); it was just a gut feeling. I saw his picture, and that was it; no pondering necessary. Max was mine!

And so, our puppy-love journey began. Devon picked him up a couple of hours away, and I prepared the apartment for meeting what I didn't know would be the most extraordinary soul of my life. I'll be honest: the first few months were tough. Max wasn't the healthiest of puppies, so I learned quickly that patience, sacrifice, and a whole lot of love are what make "mom-ing" so darn special.

Now, I love my husband, but he's not perfect. Devon had a rule that Max couldn't sleep in the bed, and I had a rule that I couldn't sleep without Max. See the problem? After two nights of my sleeping with Max on the floor, Devon tweaked his rule so that Max could sleep at the foot of the bed (so sweet of him). However, as most dogs do, Max had other plans. He quickly claimed the tip of the highest pillow as his dreamy oasis—and there he stayed.

Ahhhh, now let me tell you more about Max. He was a charming puppy—cream sable in color, with sweet brown eyes and the softest ears in the Midwest. I didn't know what a crate was and forgot I was supposed to put dogs on leashes (Dog Mom of the Year Award winner here!), so Max grew up carefully, learning his boundaries and being disciplined to know his limits. As I said before, my only pet experience was an air dog, so Max's life was a teeter-totter of trial and error, love and grace. I think that mirrors our lives as God's children, too.

Max quickly adjusted to a routine, and I quickly learned the ins and outs of being what most would call his humble servant. If you have a dog, I know you get it. He would go to class with me in my hoodie pocket, sports practice in my backpack, and every car ride perched up on my shoulder. He rarely made noise, and when he did, he made it clear that he lacked one of his basic needs.

We all soon realized that Max had four basic needs—food, water, bathroom breaks, and love. When he started getting antsy, you simply went through the list, and he would bark at his choice. It was a sight to witness. Even then, he knew what he wanted and when he wanted it. Many think this illustrates impatience, but I envy his certainty and persistence. I hope one day I will be able to navigate my life as courageously as Max—bold enough to fully be me without losing the desire to serve others. He effortlessly illustrates this daily. And let's be real, how many of us truly do that?

Now, let me backtrack a little. Our home has always had one rule, even in our pre-Max days: our front door is always open. Some say our front door is a revolving door. You are free to come and go as you please, and you are always welcome. This is truly my favorite thing about us!

Devon and I never know how many amazing guests we will have for dinner (or breakfast), and it's not something new. In college, we lived close to campus. So, instead of buying parking permits for the campus garage, our friends and their friends would squeeze into our driveway. In between classes, they would crash on our couch and grab a snack or two. We loved having friends around us and cherished the times when they became more like family.

But the best part? Max was the ultimate greeter. He loved the sound of the door opening because that meant more attention and love were coming his way. Everyone took care of Max, and he loved company. Even the cool, tough college guys would cuddle up on the couch with our little furball, and sorority girls would bring him treats from the best pet boutiques around. He simply has this charisma about him that makes you feel special, as if your company is necessary. I imagine opening the door to our small, cozy college house was similar to what heaven will feel like—a big sigh of relief because you are finally home.

As the center of our family, Max has dedicated his life to being present and has traveled many miles. One of his greatest adventures was in Washington, D.C. As a beautiful city with the most honorable history and many dog-friendly sites, we knew it would be the perfect place to take a fall trip. Max spent the trip exploring famous lawns and visiting historical monuments, like the National Mall, the Lincoln Memorial, the Washington Monument, and even a few museums.

Living life to the fullest, we filled each day to capacity. We often do that when Max is involved, and I simply love it. It's almost like an unspoken rule. We become more of who we want to be when he is there. Presence is a powerful thing, and it's proof that actions speak louder than words. He obviously never says a word, and still, you feel his love and zest for life, which fill your cup.

As you can probably tell by this point, Max is so used to being with me that when he's not, he fears I accidentally left him behind, and it's his job to save the day and reunite us. His determination is sweet but can get in the way at times. For example, for several years, Devon and I had a boat at a quaint marina on the south end of Grand Lake in Oklahoma. It wasn't overpopulated with weekenders but was full of wholesome people who loved the lake and grew to love our dogs (yes, plural, but you'll meet the others soon) like their own. It was almost magical.

Those days were filled with fish fry nights, sunrise breakfasts on the dock, and trying to soak in all the wisdom of our boat slip neighbors. It's no surprise that the best places I've been to have nothing to do with the location and everything to do with the company.

We made so many heartfelt memories at that beautiful lake with those beautiful souls. I remember one instance like it was yesterday. One afternoon at the marina, I went up the boat dock ramp to the showers across the parking lot. I left Max in the boat for his own good. Nothing made him run faster than "Max, bath time!" I was gone for maybe fifteen minutes, give or take. In the meantime, the boat was tied securely in the slip. The small space between the boat and the dock protected the vessel from weather mishaps; however, it also created a gap that had to be stepped over when exiting the boat to the dock.

Walking back down the ramp toward the slip, I immediately noticed Max wasn't in the window of the boat looking for me. I was alarmed, to say the least, so I picked up the pace and yelled his name. As I approached the boat, I heard what sounded like a fish splashing above the water. I looked down, and there was Max! It still brings tears to my eyes. He was treading water!

In Mighty Max's determination to reunite us, he'd attempted to make the heroic leap from the boat to the dock and missed. I don't know how long he had been swimming, and I still forbid my mind to wander there. I scooped him up and wrapped him in a towel. He was so tired, but I could see the relief in his eyes as if he had just swum a hundred miles to reach me. This made me wonder if God ever feels that way. Not tired of chasing us, but instantly relieved when we reach out our arms to Him. It created a whole new meaning for worshiping with my hands held high to heaven.

Oh, our adventures! From playing in the snowy mountains of Colorado to soaking up the sandy beaches of Florida, I've spent the majority of the last decade holding Max on my hip. He gives me confidence. He is the security blanket that allows me to feel bold in my own skin. Sometimes, I wonder if he knew his role was leading me to Jesus. He was my courage when I needed a Savior, and I am thankful God spoke to me in a language I was ready to understand. Seeing God's love in his beautiful brown eyes was the forever lure I needed to become the child of God I was meant to be.

Don't get me wrong—I still have moments when I question my worth. Don't we all? But then I remember that the same God who gave His Son to express His love for all of us on Earth gave me Max. So, to honor Max's life, I must honor my own.

Dogs remind me of Jesus. Their unconditional love gives us hope.

Chapter 2

LOST BUT FOUND

I have a talent: I can lose anything.

Literally, anything!

Luckily, it doesn't bother me. Well, okay, that's not entirely true. The act of losing things bothers me, but I never worry about the actual item. It's bound to turn up somewhere—usually.

My ability to lose even the most important of objects is infamous. I can lose something even when my only job is to keep track of it.

Before I tell you this story, I have to give you a little background:

I have another, let's say, quirk. Well, Devon and I both do.

We like to name things.

We'll name literally anything, from Lucy, my first vacuum, to our very small, very vintage Piper Warrior airplane, Sky Turkey. Sky Turkey flew, but that's about it. Her air conditioner was a gamble, and many times, midflight, she decided it was a heater. Cue the sweat!

Oh, yes, Sky Turkey was a gem. Compared to driving, she could get us to Grand Lake in a third of the time, so we exercised much grace for her unannounced heater tricks, paint chips, and worn-out seating. Her armrest ashtrays also threw me for a loop.

But no matter Sky Turkey's destination, we had the same routine. As co-pilot, my two jobs were choosing the most efficient altitude and serving as the official "Keeper of the Keys." As soon as we landed, my husband would hand me the plane keys. Why was this a part of the plan? I wondered that even then (because, again, my talent for losing things really knows no bounds).

Once, after a long weekend, we headed back to the airport mid-afternoon, hugged our friends one last time, moved the chalks to depart, and pulled on the door handle to load up. Except we couldn't open the door. Sky Turkey was locked, and the keys were wherever I had put them four days prior.

We searched high and low. Our friends even came back to the airport, and we retraced our entire weekend. As the night went on, we realized we were going to have to spend another night in search of the missing keys. Yes, this was a BIG OOPS on my part!

Obviously, as "Keeper of the Keys," I had failed miserably. But I decided to look in my purse one more time. I remember the car being so dark and the chilly metal brushing my fingers at the bottom of my bag.

The keys!

Of course, I wanted to find them, but not in my purse. I actually thought about throwing them on the floorboard and saying, "Hey, guys! Look! There they are!" But my heart pulled out the famous *What would Jesus do?* line. So, I prayed for mercy and sheepishly said, "Ummm, guys. I found the keys."

I'm happy to say we have very good friends—so good that every time we see them, they find a way to work in a clever comment like, "Don't give (insert the blank) to Alex; she'll put it in her purse." What they don't know is that a few months after this incident, I lost that purse, too. So, the joke's on them.

More recently, I lost my credit card while walking my Labrador, Ben. I retraced my steps over and over, but I was out of luck. I kept looking for it and monitoring my account, hoping for some clue as to the whereabouts of my most recently lost item. I never found the card, and can I just say thank goodness for online banking? Plus, I actually knew where my phone was, which is always a toss-up, so I felt pretty good, all things considered.

As I write this, I wonder, why wasn't this whole scenario more alarming to me? But as many of us do, I had a friend who went into full panic mode for me, so I had to remain somewhat calm.

Now, please understand that I don't want it to appear as if I don't worry at all. I actually worry too much in many aspects of my life. I often stress over all the little things. For example, I worry about being two minutes late for a dinner reservation. I worry about applying enough sunscreen. I worry about doing enough for others. Someone once told me that "fear not" is spoken three hundred sixty-five times in the Bible. Maybe my year would be a little better if I remembered that daily.

However, for some reason, I apparently don't worry enough about a stranger having my credit card, potentially making offshore purchases, and stealing my identity.

I have gone on to lose my passport, wallet, and every one of those little hole punch cards you get for frequently eating scoops of ice cream. It's like they know I will lose that thing before I buy ten and get one free. They just keep giving them to me, and I just keep trying to prove them wrong. As you can see, my talent is endless. Thankfully, most of the things I lose, I usually find.

But one thing I had never lost was my dog.

Until I lost my dog.

Devon and I had been saving money for some time. We were working, going to school, building businesses, and eating eggs. So many eggs! Good food is our weakness, but we knew we had bigger, better dreams coming. So, we ate eggs. They were inexpensive at the time, and I could fix them in several different ways. Every once in a while, we would splurge and top them with cheese or bacon. Such a treat!

To set the scene for you, we lived in a small, no-dogs-allowed apartment when we got Max. I know, I know. I'm a rule follower, but I feel I can share this now that the apartment building is condemned, and some very nice university townhomes sit on its soiled history.

After a month of having Max at the apartment, we moved to a storybook neighborhood. It wasn't fancy or brand new, but it was enchanting. Our street was shaded with eye-catching old trees filled with beauty and history. They knew secrets that not even the wind could tell. The sidewalks were cracked from the many miles put on them by families, college students, and game day traffic for sporting events.

It was a place where neighbors gathered in their front yards, and porch swings were full of your kids, their kids, and the kids down the block. A street where political views didn't matter and every stage of life was respected. They say it takes a village to raise a child. While that is true, it also takes a village to foster a marriage, and that street remains the foundation for my family. I learned so much there: the importance of conservation, how to get a first grader to do homework, and the meaning of *love like Jesus*. We still go back to that street for family pictures. We sit on the curb, smile, and hope our children can sense the gratitude in the air and how fresh-cut grass makes you feel at home.

Max almost instantly became a neighborhood celebrity. Everyone knew him and would come by just to say hi to our little three-pound fluff ball. He never wandered away from home, and due to physical limitations, his run was never too fast or furious. He loved to lie in the front yard, chew on small sticks, and work his magic as people walked by in awe of his color and temperament.

Max also loved to sniff everything, everyone, and everywhere. He would walk the sidewalk in front of our house, sniffing every shrub, rock, and leaf. The neighborhood was safe, and Max was too free-spirited to be limited by a leash. Besides, leashes were for dogs, and Max was neighborhood royalty.

To elaborate on his community status, Max's first birthday party was a blowout. We invited everyone we knew to the biggest "Cheeseburger in Paradise" pooch birthday bash. I don't know if you know how "cool" college students think they are, but if you can get them to wear silly-looking party hats, you know something special is going on. Everyone came. Our neighbors, their elementary school-aged sons, and people from all over the neighborhood gathered to celebrate. Our neighbors' sons brought birthday cards "signed" by their guinea pigs and illustrated with little nibble marks on the corners of the paper. Max made such an impact that when these boys graduated from high school, they sent us a card thanking us for being an important part of their child-hood. I immediately remembered Max's birthday party and wondered if they did, too.

One afternoon, in early spring, we were cleaning out flower beds and installing our sprinkler system. Let's face it; if we can eat eggs for a year, we can dig trenches for our handmade watering system. This had been an ongoing job, and Max would go outside with us daily and bask in the sun while we worked. Every few minutes, I would look up, and there he would be, lying in the soft grass, nose in the air, eyes closed as if the sunshine was his source of life. I actually catch myself doing that now. If there is a cool breeze or the first sight of the sun after rainfall, I tilt my head toward heaven, eyes closed, and think about Max's subtle ways of celebrating God's goodness.

I was a responsible dog mama. I kept a close eye on Max while he lounged in the yard. If the sun became too much, I'd spot him moving under the tree or by the porch swing. A few times, I caught him at the water bowl before returning to one of his signature spots, simply happy to be free to roam.

But one moment, he was there, and then I looked down at the dirt trenches and back up again. I scanned the yard, my eyes darting from typical Max site to typical Max site. There was no Max! Few things make me panic, but this sensation was full-out panic.

Where was he? Did an animal take him? Did someone snatch him when I wasn't looking? Did he go into the street? Oh, no. Did a car come by too fast? Why wasn't I watching him? Why did I assume he was always safe? Why? Where was he?

My voice was shaking as I yelled, "Where's Max?" I yelled for him over and over again. I used all the go-to phrases: "Max, treat!" and "Max, come!" My chest was tight, and the lump in my throat seemed to be growing as if I might suffocate. I'm sure I looked like a crazy person, running around from the front to the back yard, circling into the street and the neighbor's yard. He was not there.

Max was gone.

This was a major emergency. So, as many of us do in these dire times, I began bargaining with God and immediately realized I needed to talk to Him more. I subconsciously tried to remember the last time I thanked God for something or even the last time I wasn't praying in desperation but in appreciation. In the madness of sheer panic, I had a moment of clarity and made a mental note to be more thankful in all aspects of my life.

All of a sudden, I heard voices I recognized. My neighbors were yelling for Max. Then, I heard voices I didn't recognize. Strangers were yelling for Max. I was overwhelmed with emotion. I hadn't even had a chance to ask for help, but my community just showed up. No questions asked.

God's love wrapped around my body like a hug.

These friends and strangers didn't hesitate to assess my worth before jumping in to help. They graciously witnessed a pleading neighbor and sprang into action.

Now, I feel silly, thinking God was keeping score that day. The Lord says, "Call upon me in the day of trouble." When He saw me knee-deep in the trenches of trouble, he sent my neighbors.

In the moment, it felt as if we had searched for hours. Max wasn't just a lost dog. He was a lost family member. Knowing I would not stop until I found him, I decided to inspect the sidewalks one more time. Our neighbor had just planted a new red fire maple tree. If you don't have one, you should get one. They are easy to grow and ideal for providing shade. Famous for their deep crimson hues, their leaves graciously fall to the ground as winter approaches. Like many Oklahoma natives, I find myself drawn to the humble nature of this transitional season. The leaves of this particular tree weren't quite mature, and the dirt was still freshly tilled, loose on the surface. The shrubs surrounding its base were still there, just a little disheveled. All of a sudden, I zoned in on a tiny moving shrub.

It was Max!

There he was. In the mix of all the shrubs, fallen leaves, and dirt, he had been oblivious to my cries for his return. He had dust on his face, and the loose dirt wrapped around his paws like boots worn on the set of a Mineral City western. He was busy sniffing the new territory and getting acquainted. Following his nose to the next destination, he caught my scent and looked in my direction. There was absolutely no fear in his step, and I could feel the cortisol drain from my body as quickly as it had built.

Max's eyes locked with mine, and it was almost as if he was saying, "I'm so glad you're here, Mama! I've been waiting for you!"

Dogs remind me of Jesus.

They never ask where you've been. They simply rejoice upon your arrival.

Chapter 3

THE GARAGE

Remember your very first job? And maybe even all the silly little ones that followed?

Though they may not feel like it sometimes, I actually think they're all pretty important. I'm not so sure you get to the place you're meant to be without doing some odd jobs here and there, especially in your twenties. I know I did my fair share.

Most of us are eager to become more independent and motivated by the endless possibilities of our bright futures. And we certainly aren't nearly as tired as we are at thirty-five to forty years old!

I didn't understand that then. But I sure do now.

I would like to say I had fun side gigs like walking dogs, taste-testing foods, or lifeguarding while I soaked in some vitamin D, but I didn't have any of those "cool jobs." Instead, Devon and I sold electronics while using our home as a storage center for all kinds of gadgets. Crazy, right?

Our business grew so fast that our bedroom quickly turned into a warehouse, and most days, we couldn't even see our bed. Televisions lined the walls, and Devon was shipping them out as fast as they'd come in. We laugh at how our silly business motto, "Washing prices downstream," gave way to some of our greatest deals to date.

Another job I had consisted of going from door to door, helping people fill out US census forms. I had enough No. 2 pencils in my car to fill a small storage building. And though I never wanted to leave him behind, I didn't take Max on some of these outings because I thought they might be too dangerous for him.

Do you ever catch yourself protecting your purpose?

It's baffling when I think about it now. I was a twenty-year-old female college student going door to door at a time when cell phones didn't track location, and I was worried about my dog. Not myself—my dog! Granted, I should have been more concerned about my own well-being, but from the beginning, I recognized the significance Max would play in protecting Christ in me.

He was my tangible faith before I knew faith is better left in the heart.

Now, for a really fun one! One summer between college intersession courses, I memorized hydration facts for a popular sports drink company and had finally saved enough money to buy the required khaki pants uniform. The job description involved educating children at summer sports camps about the importance of hydration and the health effects of dehydration. However, on the first day of work, I quickly realized my actual job was to stand in my new khakis and fill up water jugs in the mud all day. The box you check stating you understand that you may be asked to lift heavy objects is real.

Never check that box.

And never wear khakis in the mud.

However, all of these experiences make me who I am today, and I love that.

Three years into college, Devon and I were searching for an endless supply of work and getting pretty good at this "odd job parade." We rarely said no to any opportunity. We painted window seals, turned a small babysitting gig into watching entire elementary classes after school, and sold parking spots in our front yard on college game days. We always said yes, regardless of our qualifications, and hoped we'd have enough time to research the task before it was go-time. The best part was that Max was welcome to tag along with us. He was always good company, and he made us appear more trustworthy.

Think about it. How threatening could two kids and a Pomeranian really be?

One of these projects was unique, though. It required us to put an epoxy coating on a neighbor's garage floor and spread decorative floor coating flakes as the surface dried. We had built a relationship with the homeowners over the last several months, as their young boys were a part of the group we watched after school. When they asked us if we were interested in the job, we quickly said yes and then went home and frantically researched how to complete such a project. It really is amazing to look back and recognize all of the things you could put on your resume but don't.

We both worked and went to school, so our availability for the job was restricted to evenings and throughout the night. Luckily, this schedule worked best with the tedious system we designed for each coat's drying calculations and flake distribution. Now, I'm going to go out on a limb here and say that chances are you didn't pick up this book to learn how to resurface your garage floor, so I'll spare you all the gritty details.

This particular project took approximately two weeks. Our friends dubbed the task "The Garage," and we liked the name. It made it much easier to tell them we couldn't go out on Friday night or to brunch on Saturday morning. "We'll be at The Garage" sounded much cooler than

"We have to go to work . . . again." And we needed all the "cool" help we could get!

Every night, we'd load up our supplies—and Max, of course—and head down the street to our neighbor's garage. We set up a little water station with all Max's essentials, and he'd sleep in a couple of drop cloths while Devon and I worked into the early hours of the morning. We'd start with a clean workspace, but as the night would go on, our paint buckets would end up in the wrong corners, and the instruction manuals would be spread out, reminding me of those large maps that unfold but never return to their neat little squares.

We were a great team! Each night, we'd get in our rhythm and transform into a two-person assembly line. We'd dream big and talk about what we were going to do with our earnings. It was always a mix of some type of investment paired with a gathering with our friends. It's a great combo if you ask me!

Did I mention we are party people? We had parties to watch television shows, parties to taste test different drinks and appetizers, and parties just because it was a Tuesday. Sometimes, we'd even calculate earnings by groceries, saying things like, "This side gig will cover the grocery bill for two weeks!" I liked doing that (and still do). The Garage was one of our more sophisticated jobs, and in terms of food, it covered groceries for several months plus a little more, which was very exciting!

Our beloved Max was becoming more and more comfortable in The Garage, and by the end of the project, he had explored most of his surroundings. On the very last night, as we sealed the final flake, we took a step back to admire our work. I feel this is a trait of all good artists. Honestly, I'm not sure why we did it, but it felt right.

It makes me wonder if God steps back to admire His work. I think it's the subtle things that would catch His eye: holding a door open for the elderly, giving a high five at a little kid's soccer game, and the joyful shrieks of two best friends seeing each other after months apart.

I believe the project doesn't have to be complete for the colors to brighten your day. So, let's start stepping back more to admire our work, our neighbors, and our friends because we are all worthy!

In this moment of celebration, we looked over and saw Max drinking water. However, his water bowl was nowhere in sight. We quickly realized that the liquid he had consumed off the garage floor wasn't made to hydrate his little body. He soon became lethargic, and the excitement in his eyes, which he often had while exploring "new land," diminished. As he laid his head on the cold garage floor, I knew I needed to act fast. I quickly scooped him up, and after assessing the situation, we headed straight to the emergency veterinarian clinic. A simple vet visit during normal hours would have sufficed, but this was the middle of the night, and our options were limited.

We spent all night and morning at the veterinarian hospital. They ran test after test, and other than a stomachache, the veterinarian determined that Max was healthy. I don't know what he drank off the garage floor, but I do know trying to figure it out cost us the entire project's wages and then some.

The job may not have made us any money, but it did bless us with unwavering friendships with our neighbors and more knowledge about concrete surfaces than I could ever want or need. When I recall every meaningful conversation and relationship we have had because of The Garage, I'd pay to coat the floor again. We've experienced projects with purpose and projects with His purpose. I'm especially thankful for the latter. I'm thankful His promise prevails over my plans every time.

Dogs remind me of Jesus.

Your best ROI (return on investment) has nothing to do with market value and everything to do with how you love others. Exponential growth looks a little different these days.

Chapter 4

BASE

Moving out of the good old college dorms—remember those glory days? So many memories . . .

A year after leaving the college dorms, Devon and I were eagerly settling into our new place. We met our neighbors and started experiencing an amazing sense of community.

Our neighborhood was simple but gorgeous. We had beautiful trees that made the autumn weather favorable, inviting front yards, and historic sidewalks popular for bicycle rides and evening strolls.

You should know I'm a big sucker for a good porch swing. I mean, deep down, who isn't? I wanted our little piece of heaven to have a porch swing, but there was only one problem: we didn't have a porch.

Why was this a big deal? Well, let me explain. During my junior year of college, I was invited to join an athletic leadership council for my D1 sport, and to celebrate, Devon gifted me my first porch swing. When I got home from practice, he had it set up under the tree in our front yard. Max was already snuggled on the pillow of the seat, and I knew "our place" had just been created. I love how places can bring you closer to God, and the company often solidifies the notion.

The best part about that swing was the fellowship it invited. It quickly became a community swing, and I loved coming home to our friends lounging in the shade, neighbors catching up after a day of chaos at work, or neighborhood kids reading their first chapter books curled up in the middle seat. It seemed as though everyone loved my swing—and Max. Oftentimes, someone would knock on the door, asking if Max could come outside to the swing. I wonder how many people sat there with Max, just sitting. Pausing. Breathing in the stillness and exhaling the unnecessary.

We even had a few yard sales with our neighbors over the years, and the swing was always the cashier's domain. I also ate countless lunches there, sitting next to Max and listening to the campus bell tower chimes. If home could be heard, that was it.

It was often the "home base" in the neighborhood kids' games of tag, which became more extraordinary to me over time as I realized the old porch swing was my home base as well. We tend to be drawn toward comfort in times of worry and uncertainty. Have you ever seen a mother with a toddler wrapped around her legs, peeking out from behind them? Or watched a teenager slam their bedroom door out of frustration? Have you ever witnessed a friend deep in sorrow, wrapped in their favorite blanket? What about a young girl in her twenties, holding her dog on a porch swing?

Home base can look very different for many of us. I just pray your base is a safe, comfortable place that allows your worries to flow out and God to flow in.

No one ever made a big deal about my swing. It was just a beautiful place we all subconsciously cherished. After we turned the house into a rental property and moved, I assumed I was the only one upon whom it had left such a fond impression. I'd talk to Devon about memories here or there and the significant pull that spot had on my heart. Every year, Devon would say, "What do you want for your birthday?" This was a tough question for me. To this day, gifts make me feel uncomfortable, so I'd rather have one hundred birthday cards. However, about six years after we moved, Devon asked yet again, "What do you want for your birthday?"

Without hesitation, I said, "I want to swing with Max."

So, as a surprise, Devon and Max set up a porch swing under that same historic oak tree, and I swung with my baby in the cold February wind like it was late summer fading into autumn football weather.

That memory will live on in my mind forever. I don't even remember which birthday it was, but I hope to experience many more special days in my lifetime, just like that one.

A few years ago (and almost fifteen years after the purchase of that first porch swing), we went on vacation with our porch-swing neighbors, whose children were now the age I was when I got that old swing. The vacation wasn't anything elaborate or spectacular. It was just a getaway at an old beach house, but we spent our time reminiscing about the "good ol' days."

Then, in a passing conversation, our former neighbor said, "Hey, remember that old porch swing?" I wish I had shared in the moment how the swing had been a pivotal element in my spiritual journey, and how each friend and neighbor who sat there illustrated God's intention of bringing people together.

I didn't.

I wish I could have cried out about how grateful my heart felt not to carry the significance alone.

Yet, I didn't.

I wish I could have just simply said, "I loved that old thing."

But I didn't. I let water fill my eyes for just a moment, and then I smiled quickly before the conversation naturally continued. It feels good not to be alone, and sometimes, there are no words for feelings that powerful.

When we went to bed that night, I curled up with my back to the middle. Devon leaned over me and wrapped his arm around my shoulders. He whispered, "Alex, did you hear her tonight? She loved the porch swing, too." As I let my body be comforted by his warm embrace, I closed my eyes and sank into my home base.

Dogs remind me of Jesus.

Love will always lead you home.

Chapter 5

BRONCO RIDES

Meet Zeus.

Zeus was the poster dog for all Labradors.

He was the Roy Rogers of the Wild West, your favorite Beatle from the 1960s, and the modern-day YouTube sensation. Well, wait, let me rewind just a bit.

Devon's family bought Zeus in the country for two hundred dollars, and before I share anything else, I can say with one hundred percent confidence that it was the best investment the Millers ever made.

Reflecting on his childhood, Devon said he chose Zeus because Zeus was accidentally injured during the process of his mother caring for the large litter. She had picked him up by the cheek, which left Zeus with a permanent scar under his eye—his battle scar, if you will. It's fascinating that, at an early age, what Devon saw in Zeus wasn't labeled as a weakness but characterized as an illustration of resilience. I'm sure God sees the same thing in us; we aren't damaged—we are renovated.

Now, I obviously wasn't there, but from what I've been told, Zeus was not an easy puppy. The local golf course would call several times a week, informing the Miller family that Zeus had spent the day there, stealing golf balls, digging holes, and making messes. It makes me giggle just thinking about it.

But above all the dirt, messes, and disasters, Zeus was loyal. He loved in a way that brought the Miller family together. So, they'd load up in the truck and go get him. The Miller boys' childhood memories mostly involve boats, water, and Zeus.

Growing up, a relative lived across the cove from them, and sometimes, Zeus would swim to her house with at least one of the boys holding on to his tail. You could say that he was the ultimate watercraft. He'd swim miles in a day, catching snacks from neighbors and living a pirate's dream. As time went on, Zeus became a crowd favorite and the center of the community. Some of Devon's happiest moments were watching Zeus follow the school bus to school.

But life happens.

As the Miller boys grew up, so did Zeus. Before long, his best mates were off to college. Sadly, we all know that dogs age much quicker than humans, and Zeus was ready for retirement shortly after Devon graduated from college.

After living a full life on the water, the famous Grand Lake canine packed his favorite treats and toys and moved to the city to live with Devon and me. City life was a tough adjustment, and Zeus found himself on many strange front porches, waiting for me to arrive. Just as the Miller family had always done, we'd load up and go get him.

Zeus was an old dog learning new tricks and experiencing new things.

When Zeus moved in with us, he had many firsts. He went for a walk on the sidewalk with a leash. He learned about dog parks, which he completely embraced in his own unique way. Unlike his other furry counterparts, Zeus ignored every dog there and instead went to a human and sat at their feet until they acknowledged him. Then, he'd make his way to the next person, get some love, and move on.

The dog park also had a large pond.

So, one day, Zeus took it upon himself to swim across it. When he realized he didn't have an exit plan on the other side, he just made a big loop and swam back. Apparently, he was the first dog to make such a daring loop. The other dog lovers there vocalized their concerns when he reached the middle. They had obviously never seen a true water dog like our Zeus.

Another first for Zeus was experiencing a bath. Now, let me start by saying that I had no real experience bathing large animals either. I could bathe Max in the sink in five minutes flat, but that is where my bathing expertise ended. Washing Zeus required a whole different level of patience, strength, and talent. So, as any good dog mama would do, after a few painful attempts at what seemed like civilizing Tarzan, I made him an appointment with a professional.

Zeus never shied away from adventure. He swam with ease, explored from dusk to dawn, and rode shotgun in Devon's Ford Bronco with his ears flapping in the breeze. Our 1990 Bronco is special—not to mention it's the absolute perfect truck for driving around, windows down, with a handsome Labrador smiling out the back window.

This old (but cherished) Ford has a long history with Devon and is still an iconic piece in our household. He bought the truck when he turned sixteen and was exceedingly proud of it. He drove it around everywhere with the windows down, the music loud, and the fuel gauge always just a sliver above empty.

But before Devon went to college, he decided to sell it. As you can probably guess, this was a terrible idea!

A few weeks after the transaction, he couldn't take the heartbreak and had to buy it back. He didn't believe anyone else could possibly appreciate it like he did, and I'm pretty sure he paid more for it the second time around—although he still won't admit to it.

I'll attest that our beloved Bronco has a solid history within our family. This truck took us on many dates as a young couple. (Oh, the good old days!) It played music while we danced in restaurant parking lots. The first car door Devon ever opened for me belonged to the Bronco.

At times, it was deemed "The Lake Truck" and hauled countless wet dogs home after beautiful days on the water. It also weathered a period of being "The Airport Car." It would sit at a small hangar at Grand Lake Airport and shuttle us to and from the boat after flying for the weekend. The entire flight, we'd pray the old truck would start once we landed in Northeast Oklahoma. We would keep jugs of oil in the back to replenish the poor thing every couple of months (or days), depending on how often we drove it.

Like us, Zeus loved riding in the Bronco.

He loved the windows down and the simplicity of just loading up—no need for rules or seat covers. Fortunately for him, it was the only car we had that would hold him comfortably. So, a friend and I loaded him up in the old ride and took him to his first grooming appointment.

He was in for a treat. We promised him we'd be back soon and dropped him off for a wash. We ran some errands and, as promised, returned a couple of hours later to pick him up.

The shop's aroma was perfect for this quaint doggie washing establishment, equal parts lavender and wet fur. Have you ever noticed how all these places have the same scent? The receptionist was welcoming, and we paid the fee as the grooming assistant went to retrieve Zeus from the back.

She brought him out, and man, did he look different! I knew he had been a tad dirty, but this clean lad didn't look a thing like the pup I brought into the shop. On the way to the truck, I mentioned to my friend that I had never seen Zeus look so clean, fresh, and almost regal. I was impressed, but I still felt like I didn't even recognize him.

We made our way to the truck and assumed our positions at the Bronco. My friend came to assist me because, while Zeus was a mighty lake dog, sometimes, his knees didn't cooperate, and he needed a little help loading himself into the back of the Bronco. It was a two-person job, for sure. She would always "bear hug" him around his chest, and I would pick up his back end. However, as soon as I bent down to hug his torso, I gasped.

I said, *"This doesn't look like Zeus because it's NOT Zeus!"*

The groomer had mistakenly given us someone else's dog. I couldn't believe it. Only something this ridiculous would happen to me. I know this could have been an unnerving situation, but it wasn't. I knew in my heart that Zeus was safe inside. So, I took a big breath and hauled the look-alike dog back inside the building.

To say they were mortified would be an understatement. They apologized profusely (at least a hundred times) and went to fetch Zeus, the original.

Zeus didn't mind one bit. He was happy to see us despite having watched us leave with an impostor. He'd just waited patiently for us to return. He was confident in my pause and didn't let it obstruct his purpose. He knew we'd be back.

God does, too.

You can never be gone too long. I love that about dogs. I love that about God, too. How would my life have progressed if I had never let God's pauses obstruct my purpose? If something isn't going your way, like a big promotion or whatever it may be, sometimes it's the pause that's preparing you for something greater. Changing direction or course isn't a failure. Renewal is not rejection, and a season of rest is not God's refusal. I need to take note of that more on a daily basis.

Now, let's fast forward.

Several years later, I had just gotten Ben, our second Lab. Devon and I, along with some friends, were headed to a furniture store after renting a big van to haul our latest purchases. We didn't have much room for extra items, but I still spent at least an hour trying to figure out how to fit baby Ben's crate in the back.

I'll be honest: I had packed like we were going on a week-long trip instead of a day-long outing. I had Ben's food, water bowls, and favorite blankets. I had also gone back into the house a few times to grab some very important items, like his new toy and the light-up leash. (Have you ever seen a light-up leash? It's not necessary, but it sure is fun!) Finally, after watching me continue to finagle with the crate, my dog-loving friend asked, "Just out of curiosity, why are we taking Ben again?"

I looked at her, dumbfounded. I had no idea. I couldn't think of a reasonable answer. My mind went back to the grooming story with Zeus.

I had almost loaded the *wrong* dog for the *right* reasons, and now, I was loading the *right* dog for the *wrong* reasons. In my mind, I was simply trying to show my little Ben how much I cared. Everyone knew how much I loved Max, and I didn't want Ben to ever be second best.

Luckily, that's not how love is measured.

And thankfully, my friend helped me make sense of it all. So, I unloaded the dog crate and kissed Ben goodbye. He didn't need to be hauled around with me that day for him to know I loved him. Love doesn't turn on and off like a light switch. I was forgetting all the little things, the day-to-day engagements that foster consistent commitment.

Looking back, I was forgetting all the times Zeus had placed his nose literally one millimeter from my face in the middle of the night and let out a short, low bark because he needed to go outside. I'd awaken startled but still graciously get up and open the back door. I was forgetting the moments when Ben would be too tired to finish our walks, and I'd carry him home. I was forgetting the countless nights when I'd stumbled to the bathroom after being asleep for a few hours and, on the way back to bed, made a "sleeping dog pit stop" to kiss him one more time on the forehead. Have you ever noticed Labradors have the perfect brow ridge for forehead kissing? I've never met a Lab that didn't have this perfect snuggle structure.

I suddenly realized that Ben's worth wasn't going to be jeopardized if I left him at home for an afternoon, and my worth wasn't going to be condemned if I spent the afternoon without him. This whole concept was so freeing!

To this day, I'm trying to be more mindful of the consistent small actions that keep life less chaotic and more steadfast. My guilt over one moment shouldn't minimize the magnitude of my merit. Why do I keep score with myself? Why do we tally our errors over our accomplishments? None of it is really necessary.

You can hop in the car on a Sunday afternoon, windows down, music up, and your dog riding shotgun. Or not. Maybe you leave your pup at home, only to return hours later for cuddles on the couch. Both are enough. No scorecard, no agenda, just you and your best friend inhaling fresh air and exhaling steadfast love.

Dogs remind me of Jesus.

They don't keep score.

A dog's loyalty isn't based on your goodness but theirs. I only wish we could see our hearts like they do because I know that's how He does, too.

Chapter 6

EVERYONE'S BEST FRIEND

Zeus was family. We'd do anything for him.

Remembering Zeus's resilience, I think we all naively assumed everything would be okay when a growth appeared on the bridge of his spine. Many things changed over the next year. Zeus had surgery on his back, and the long and painful recovery process took a toll on all of us. I learned how to dress significant wounds in the middle of the night and, more importantly, how to pray to a God I was just getting to know.

Being his nurse during those difficult times still feels like one of my greatest honors. Our veterinarian was a remarkable man, and while he removed much of the tumor, we knew there were parts he couldn't extract without paralyzing our beloved Labrador. No one could say how long it would take for the tumor to grow back, so we decided we would only put him through the operation one time. Luckily, we didn't really have to make the decision. Medically, it was a one-time surgery from the beginning. Zeus healed and, for several months, was moving better and getting into his typical city mischief, which made us smile.

Zeus usually slept upstairs in our bedroom, but as the growth began increasing in size again, he started struggling with the stairs. Eventually, Zeus couldn't make it to the bedroom without crying. At this time, we moved our pillows and blankets to the couch to sleep by him for the remainder of his life. If Zeus taught us anything, it was that we are a family, and family is loyal. We were in this together.

Maybe that is God's ultimate plan—bringing people together regardless of the situation.

As the days passed, Zeus grew sicker. We were at a loss. We slept on the couch, occasionally hand-feeding him and giving him little boosts to help him get up and go outside. Zeus was our first senior dog, so we turned to others for advice. We decided to start celebrating him daily and began planning for his fourteenth birthday party.

Celebrating life is a huge part of who we are!

We love celebrations, and Zeus's special day was no different. For number fourteen, we went all-out-surprise style! We invited all his canine friends, and before long, the backyard was full of pups in party hats—and, more importantly, their owners, the most gracious friends you could ever find. As I brought Zeus around the corner in his new bandana and "Birthday Boy" pin, everyone yelled, "Surprise!" They all played along so well, and in moments like these, you truly realize what God meant by "love thy neighbor."

On that day, I knew in my heart that Zeus truly had the best time. He had special ice cream and cake from a dog bakery, and his friends brought him all the treats and toys he could imagine. In those few hours, Zeus was a puppy again, and I felt like I was in the king's backyard. Zeus's fourteenth is a celebration we still talk about to this day.

I think it's an understated indication that gifts from God aren't earned. Worth isn't warranted by numerical value. Devon and I didn't have ten dogs and their owners in our backyard that day because we deserved it. They were all true gifts in our lives that God knew we needed at that moment. We hold onto these memories because, along the way, Zeus's loyalty became a reflection of who we all wanted to be. Looking around the backyard that day, I realized Zeus was everyone's best friend.

March 11 – The Celebration
Happy Birthday, Zeus!

.....

March 25 – It's Springtime

Spring is here! The red birds are singing. Boaters begin de-winterizing their vessels.

.....

April 10 – Nature is Beautiful
The sun is shining. The flowers are blooming.
The lake water is warming up.

…..

A few months later, spring was in full swing. I still remember it like it was yesterday.

Devon was out of town, and I planned to meet him the next day. I came home from work, and Zeus wasn't well. He was lying down, and it took all I had to pick him up and help him down the porch stairs to the backyard. I remember looking into his eyes and seeing the unbearable pain he was enduring. It shattered my heart into a million pieces.

I knew it was time.

After calling Devon, we both agreed that Zeus's happiness and well-being came first, above everything else. An hour later, a friend helped me take Zeus to the veterinary office. We brought his special fourteenth birthday bed, and I lay with him. I wanted him to feel comfortable and safe, the same way he had made us feel all those years.

I didn't know what else to do, so I just talked to him, as we always had. I told him I would miss him and that he'd made me a better wife, mother, and person. I simply wanted to say thank you. I didn't know if he understood my words, so I just kept telling him I loved him and that he was a good boy.

He was the ultimate "good boy."

I truly believe you don't always need the right words. Sometimes, you just need to be there, fully present in the moment. So, there I was, lying in a dog bed, holding a legend, wondering how in the world God ever thought I was good enough to be Zeus's mom.

Zeus entered my life as a blessing and left as a bigger blessing, impacting my life for years to come.

For many years, Zeus's special box was placed by the captain's chair on our boat. It has a nice, shiny label with his name and the phrase, "Everyone's Best Friend." It really is the only way to describe him.

It's amazing what a dog can do for a community. I've never seen an animal have so many people on his team. Grace can do some remarkable things, and if it takes a dog to show me God's love, then sign me up. Sign me up for the holes on the golf course, the late-night swims, dressing wounds at midnight, and lying on the finest dog bed in the middle of a cold vet office, holding the paw of the best friend I'll ever know.

Sign me up for all of it. Zeus was worth it. I'd love to load up and go get him today.

After two years of missing Zeus, I still found myself crying in heartache. Gosh, I missed that dog! We had just moved again and added a new puppy, Ben, to our family that winter. I remember having a bad day and walking outside in the spring air. The flowers were blooming, and I could smell the fresh-cut grass. The sun hit my face in a way I had never felt. I closed my tear-stained eyes, tilted my head toward heaven's sky, and openly talked to God for the first time.

I said, "God, just give me a sign. Let me know he is with you, and free me of this guilt. Please, give me a sign that Your grace is enough, and His love lives on."

As I opened my eyes, blurry from the morning light, a red bird fluttered onto the tree in front of me. Maybe it was because Zeus always wore a red collar, but without thinking, I bowed my head and said, "Hi, Zeus." With those words, a grateful smile crept across my face.

A few years later, a colleague of mine explained how the red bird is represented in her native culture. To my surprise, they symbolize loved ones in heaven. It may be the biggest coincidence of my life, but I'll take it.

God was speaking my language, and I am so thankful I was listening.

In hindsight, my biggest regret is not getting to know God more while Zeus was alive because I'm sure I could have loved him better. I'm certain he would have wagged his tail forever, regardless of the discomfort he was enduring. He held on so we wouldn't hurt, but that was not his purpose. His purpose was all the joy, life lessons, and love he gave us. It was to fill our hearts with unconditional love. This taught me about the misconception that Jesus saves us from pain, but Jesus never promised that. He came to save our souls, not our bodies, from the pain we endure as humans. I had to accept that I couldn't save Zeus from the pain, and prolonging mine was no longer beneficial.

Dogs remind me of Jesus.

They don't come to rescue us from pain but to save our faithful hearts.

Chapter 7

HI, FRIEND

Friend. BFF. Kindred spirit.

We bestow these titles upon the special people (or pets) in our lives.

After Zeus died, a friend's dog had puppies, and Devon said that if one looked like Zeus, we could adopt him. Nine puppies were born … and no sign of one looking like Zeus. Then, several hours later, Ben was born. My friend called me immediately because his markings were just like Zeus's.

When Ben was presented to me, he was wearing a little blue striped shirt that read, "World's Best Friend." I giggle at the thought of how it had draped over him like a king-sized comforter. Now, I'm not even sure it could fit over his paw.

Ben must have thought his clothing gave purpose to his life's work. I know he truly believes "World's Best Friend" is his official title because, throughout his life, he has proven over and over that he is the ultimate BFF. The special thing about Ben's friendship is that he doesn't play favorites. He has this abundant love, and there's always enough for everyone. I feel like selfless love multiplies like that. If Ben could talk, "Hi, Friend" would be his favorite saying. He has the ability to make you feel as if you are the only person in the room while simultaneously being eager to add other friends to the mix.

It's difficult to describe, but people just love Ben. I'll put it this way: Any time we go on a vacation and need a babysitter for our two young daughters, people hide in the woods as if they are going to be chosen as the next Hunger Games tribute. I'll admit that it's a fair response. I try to hide sometimes, too, but they can sniff me out (probably because of all the extra time they spend with dogs).

However, when we go on vacation and need a dog sitter for Ben, we could hire a secretary to sift through all the pleading phone calls from our friends, each one boasting the qualifications that make them more qualified than the next to watch our baby Ben. I've never seen a group of people throw each other under the bus so quickly.

When we moved across the country, I couldn't count the endless conversations I had confirming, "Yes, we are taking Ben," and "No, Ben can't stay." I still get random messages asking if Ben can come back to visit for the weekend. My response? "No, Ben is a dog. He can't fly alone," and "No, he needs his mama at night." The latter is true, but probably not as much as I like to believe. He's just easy to love because he loves everyone.

It makes me wonder how influential we would be if love was our only agenda, too.

Now, I must say Ben loves people, but he also loves dogs. He's definitely the "the more, the merrier" type. At Grand Lake, Ben is fully in his element. Ben was born in January, and as soon as the temperature rose above freezing, he was running into the waves and jumping off the dock. The marina was brimming with fellow slip renters and, best of all, more furry friends.

From the dock, he could hear the slightest creak of a car door and would run up the ramp to see which lake bum neighbor had arrived. Lake people love the water, and luckily, they also love dogs. So, Ben was eager to play with whichever pooch was riding shotgun with their parents. Most furry friends were delighted to receive his greeting of a few sniffs and a "Hey, catch me if you can."

However, some were not. Ben is smart, but he could never tell the difference between "It's so good to see you, too" and "Please give me space."

One recurring situation we had to manage involved a dog known to run the dock. He was one-third the size of Ben but had three times the might. He was older and had accrued more dockhand years than Ben. There was no question—he was in charge. Usually, he was friendly, but *not* to Ben.

He took Ben's enthusiasm as a threat and acted accordingly. It never failed: every week, this tiny pup would trot down to the dock, and every week, Ben would get a rude awakening right to the muzzle. Despite his unfriendliness, Ben was drawn to him. We literally couldn't keep him away from this little dog.

Ben would hear him coming and just couldn't help but give him one more chance. It was never a truly unsafe situation, but that little dog would scare Ben so much that he'd come yelping back to the boat. Still, he would never linger on the side of caution. A new week, a new chance.

It's really interesting when you think about it. I sit back and ponder all the times I've struck out because my pride preceded my purpose. How many times would a clean slate have saved my day? Or your day?

Ben has never truly understood the magnitude of his size. He has always been "Baby Ben." Ironically, we had a Pomeranian who insisted he was a Labrador and a Labrador who was certain he was a teacup-sized Pom. Ben slept in an extra-small dog bed for several years until his paws became as big as the bed. As a puppy, he always wanted to be on my lap—close was not close enough. He had zero spatial awareness, but I loved every second of it.

Knowing he would grow exceedingly fast, we had many rules and boundaries for Ben. The biggest one? He was not allowed on the furniture, especially our bed. During those first few weeks, though, we would wake up in the middle of the night, and somehow, Ben would have oh-so-quietly curled up under our arms or nestled himself just perfectly into our necks. He just wanted to be included.

Don't we all?

What I loved most was that Ben displayed his delicate side long before we brought him home. Before I adopted Ben, I helped take him and his nine littermates to get vaccinations and checkups with my dear friend, who thought her dog would only have a few puppies. Of course, a few puppies turned out to be ten, and we found ourselves with a laundry basket full of would-be flying squirrels headed to the veterinary office. Note to self: get a basket with a lid next time.

It was a standard appointment, and each pup was examined and given the proper immunizations. One by one, no issues, until it was Ben's turn. He cried and squealed like it was complete torture: the touch of the cold stethoscope, a baby fine needle, those scary-looking lab coats with endless pockets. *What did they keep in there, anyway? It surely wasn't a treat.*

I carried his delicate, loving soul back to the waiting area because he just couldn't bear to walk. He burrowed his little body into mine, inspiring a swarm of mama's boy jokes that have followed him around his entire life. From the beginning, he was labeled over-sensitive and (gasp!) a fraidy cat.

But what if more of us could bravely wear our hearts on our sleeves like Ben? Not in an overly offended sense, but in a more abundantly authentic style. It makes empathy seem a lot more necessary in everyday life.

People say Ben fears everything. While that may be a little bit of an exaggeration, I partially agree. What makes Ben special, though, is that his distress never exceeds his love. Fear never holds him back from loving without reservation. I wonder sometimes . . . What if people could be more like Ben?

I believe that more dinner tables would be full of laughter, more families would enjoy Sunday afternoons in the park, and life would be a little more peaceful.

Dogs remind me of Jesus.

They'll approach without reservation because God's children deserve grace.

Chapter 8

BETTER BEN

Love is patient. Love is kind. Love multiplies.

And so do bananas! (I'm just kidding—obviously, that's not how the verse goes!)

But it's true in this case. I don't mean to toot my own horn, but I grew banana trees in Oklahoma that actually produced fruit. No joke! I had bananas growing in my house in the blistering cold of an Oklahoma December.

Ask anyone, and they'll tell you it's true. I literally went around all winter saying, "Hey, I grew bananas!" I told our friends, fellow shoppers in the grocery store line, and anyone who would roll down their window at a traffic stoplight. These bananas multiplied rather quickly, and before long, anyone who came over for dinner took a party favor of one new banana sprout home with them.

The truth is, I knew nothing about growing banana trees. *GASP!*

As I would with any houseplant, I watered them, gave them light, and relocated them into nice ceramic planters for the winter months. However, I always believed my secret was talking to them. Give them a little water and a "You're doing great!" and pretty soon, you'll have prize bananas, too.

Reflecting back on this experience, I realize I just provided what I thought I would need to grow—resources, light, and supportive company—and made it more "a-peeling" to banana trees. (See what I did there?)

Each year, I moved my plants outside, inside, and outside again. Why didn't I have a greenhouse? Great question. These planters were so heavy that our friends refused to see us when the seasons changed. As my collection grew, I had to get creative—I mean, *really* creative—to recruit help.

I'd make pounds of biscuits and gravy, secret ingredient cupcakes, and offer movers' choice refreshments. If your friends aren't motivated by home-cooked meals, do you even know what a good time is? The best part of my negotiation tactics was that these friends were going to show up regardless of the gravy status. Our "true family"—while not necessarily blood—showed up to carry the weight, even when it was too heavy. And that's what makes life so special.

I realize my plants were often too heavy, so this is my public thank you to anyone who has ever helped move, drag, or slide a Miller family planter.

As you can imagine, these "moves" gave way to so many amazing memories. My husband and his best friend always think they have the best ideas. So, a few months after my banana success, I earned this reputation as a plant connoisseur, which was neither valid nor desired. On a separate note, Devon had a couple of Ficus trees outside his office. Standing seven feet tall with a circumference wider than three Labradors following each other like elephants, these trees were deteriorating quickly.

So, these two highly educated men decided to load these trees into temporary planters and bring them to our house—by house, I mean inside. And did I mention they failed to tell me they were bringing them?

Some surprises are good. *Some are not.*

These weeping figs shed more leaves than Ben does hair. I'd wake up and sweep up leaves, come home from work and sweep up leaves, and right before bed, I'd sweep up leaves one more time. I should probably repent for all the things I thought about the "tree deliverers" during these times.

Once again, resources, light, and encouragement brought these weeping figs out of dormant despair, and it seemed as if they literally grew overnight. I can think of a few times when resources, light, and compassionate company turned my life around overnight, too. Can you?

But finally, it was time.

After I convinced the guys to get those trees out of the house, they informed me that they were too big to move. So, these brilliant men brought a chainsaw into the house and trimmed the branches just enough to get them out the door and back to the office. After that, I never saw those men, I mean trees, again.

So clearly, my plant collection was growing, and so was our puppy, Ben.

Labradors are known for their temperament and intelligence. They are also known to be puppies for a long time. Luckily, potty training Ben was a breeze. However, teaching Ben self-control was not. He was impulsive yet remorseful, and we struggled to find that delicate balance between giving him the freedom to practice willpower and setting strict boundaries to protect our belongings.

Ben wasn't interested in getting in the trash, but he was always down for tearing up paper products. He ate countless rolls of toilet paper, could find napkins I didn't even know we had, and retired many books in my library collection.

One day, I was reading a beautiful book about the life of Jesus. I had started it a few days before and had told everyone it should be their next read. When I came home, I found that Ben had eaten the front cover, the epilogue, and about four of those insert pictures the authors put in the middle for visual aids. At that moment, I remember thinking Ben must hate me and the Lord because who would willingly eat a picture of the Last Supper?

But what can you do? I put all the paper goods on high shelves, and a few weeks later, I decided to give Ben another chance. This time, as I hugged the cutest Labrador on the planet and then left for work, I was confident in his self-control abilities. Oops! I never would have guessed that hours later, I would come home to a blue Smurf.

Either Ben had just come from Blue Man Group tryouts, or something was very wrong. He was covered in blue ink, head to toe. I was startled, confused, and intrigued all at the same time. As I walked into the house, I noticed the living room rug looked suspiciously like Ben's new body paint. After more sleuthing, I discovered Ben had found extra ink cartridges in the office, opened them in the living room, and proceeded to paint everything in his path. His creativity knew no bounds!

I once had a little boy ask me, "Does Ben really know right from wrong?" The simple answer is yes, but that wrongly implies he does the right thing the majority of the time. By now, we all know Bad Ben isn't perfect. I answered, "Yes," and followed it with a big, "BUT . . ."

"Yes, he does, *BUT* he still makes mistakes. He is learning. And that's good enough for me."

God must think the same thing about us.

We normally know the right thing to do, but often, we choose the easy way out. I can imagine His pride when, the second time around, we choose to be noble. I'm thankful His grace gives me the freedom to make choices and the autonomy to try again. He's not there to give commands, but He's always there to give mercy.

And if one word was needed to survive Ben's puppy-like behavior, it was *mercy*.

Devon's grace for Ben ended way before mine. I remember it clear as day. We had just watered the indoor plants before work. Among the banana trees were numerous other tropical plants in heavy (but not weeping fig heavy) ceramic planters. Ben had proven some growth in self-discipline and was left out to roam for the day.

I returned during lunch to check on him. Ben always met me at the door, but not today. Cue the warning alarms. He was hiding in his crate, and I don't know what was hiding him better—his blanket or the mud covering his entire body. I quickly let him out the back door and went to inspect the damage.

Somehow, our house had withstood a tropical tidal wave brought on by Hurricane Ben. The planters, which were on wheels, had been pulled down the stairs. Most of our plants had been pulled up by their roots and strung throughout the living area. If palm leaves could run through a paper shredder, that was what our kitchen was decorated with. It was leafy chaos!

Due to the watering schedule earlier in the day, where there would have been dirt, there was now mud. Mud coated every surface where Ben had jumped, run, and played. And by the looks of his not-so-small tracks, this wasn't a lounging-by-the-window kind of morning. I imagine the sound of the broken flowerpots startled him, and while running for his life, Ben slipped on some mud. As you can imagine, the rest is history.

When Devon arrived home, I was replanting salvageable foliage and cleaning that ink-stained rug for the second time. I'll never forget his face when he said (not-so-calmly), "Take that dog to a behavioral class now! If this isn't better by tomorrow, Max and I are putting him on Craigslist."

It still makes me giggle. Sometimes, Devon uses Max when he thinks I'll say no or disagree, but he's still serious. "Max and I want to know if you want to watch a movie." "Should we buy this car? Max wants it." So, I knew he meant business, and I immediately called the veterinarian's office in desperation. I said, "I need to see your behavioral specialist. If I don't get Ben help today, my husband's going to put him on Craigslist!"

I could tell there were a few smiles on the other end of the line (I bet you're smiling now, too), and they let me bring him right away. I told them the story, his impulsive ways, and how he had dubbed the nickname Bad Ben in such a short time. Ben just sat, good-boy style, listening and not moving a muscle. Of course, they pointed out how his current demeanor didn't match his reputation, and we left with a handful of treats and a few tips to make this stage manageable.

Time is a beautiful thing.

Throughout the years, Ben has grown into the best-behaved dog. He seldom barks, never jumps on people or furniture, and loves kids like a true protector. Luckily, his paper-eating days are far behind him. When we reflect on his past as Bad Ben, people are quick to defend him. His past doesn't define him. I wonder how our lives would be different if we took grace in stride like Ben, forgave each other more, forgave ourselves more, and didn't let shame hold us back. Ben has now earned the name Better Ben, and I know my life would be a whole lot better if I could be more like him.

Ben's love overshadows all. All his little tics and negative behavioral habits—everything—and trust me, he still has some. He won't walk outside in the rain. He refuses to touch wet grass, and if the grass needs to be mowed yesterday, he won't even tiptoe on it.

I wish I could love so big that people just overlooked all my odd tendencies and apprehensions. I wish I could love so much that no one ever noticed that I hate the mere idea of water on my neck (maybe that's where Ben gets it) or that I like to eat popcorn in bed regardless of the mess. Also, I need a lot of love because my singing ability is nonexistent (Shhhhh!), so let's overlook that, too.

Do you ever wonder why we can't love that big? I wonder what keeps us from loving so wildly that the background never overshadows the eminent goodness within.

Dogs remind me of Jesus.

We don't have to be perfect to be truly loved.

Chapter 9

OL' RED

Gorgeous lake views, warm sunshine, uninterrupted family and friend time—do you have some of those good ol' memories, too?

Grand Lake o' the Cherokees is nestled in the northeastern corner of Oklahoma, separating farmland from fishermen and out-of-towners. Most of Grand Lake rests in Grove, Oklahoma, where the population of the small town nearly doubles during the summer—not even joking!

The marinas are filled with crawfish boils, tiki bars, and fried fish that only a family friend you've known forever can fry better. Fishing tournaments lure water lovers from all over, and city kids flock to the yacht clubs for every big holiday. Water sports, ideal sailing conditions, and bass tournaments attract those escaping the summer heat. It's a beautiful thing.

Southern hospitality is a remedy to the long winters in metropolitan areas, causing visitors to continue to pour in year after year. Owning property on the lake is a captain's dream, and if you're fortunate enough to witness the Duck Creek Fireworks from your dock, you have truly made it in life. Independence Day is the busiest day of the year, and boats flood into the south end of the lake for the biggest fireworks display in Oklahoma. It's magical, to say the least.

They say lake life is the best life—and I agree.

Devon grew up driving boats and mowing shorelines, living in a very water-oriented world. My love for the water came later, born from the wind in my hair and the look on fourteen-year-old Devon's face when we watched the Duck Creek fireworks while semi-holding hands. To be honest, I don't remember what life was like before embracing the simple joys of glistening lake water, but I can't imagine it being this much fun.

Lake life has me hooked. From twelve hundred miles away, our summers still revolve around a trip to Grand Lake for the fireworks show. It's the simple fun that's often lost in the bustle of everyday life.

As our family grew, one dog at a time, the lake continued to be a safe haven. When I was gifted my Labrador

Retriever, Ben, I remember thinking, *I can't wait to take him swimming. Wait, what if he doesn't like the water?* I had to stay positive. He was part of our family, so of course, he would like the water—I hoped.

It was a long winter full of anticipation for his first lake trip. Luckily, we were two for two, and both of our pups enjoyed the refreshing, cool water of summertime. You know you have found the perfect Pomeranian when he jumps off the boat like an All-American Labrador! I find it kind of funny. The poor thing doesn't know any better, and I love that about him.

We had it all: the boat, the water dogs, and the flawless bowline, but apparently, we were missing one thing.

So, we bought a shiny red kayak.

Okay, well, my husband secretly bought a kayak while I sat on a mall park bench waiting for him to pick me up, but that's a fight—I mean, story—for another time. The weight limit on the kayak was two hundred forty pounds, which was perfect. Devon pictured taking it out early in the mornings, drinking coffee while our Pomeranian guided the way.

I must add that Max is a great passenger. When he rides in the front of the kayak, we like to believe he magically transforms into Maxopher Columbus. Poised on his back legs with his nose in the air, Max could conquer the world in that small boat.

I envisioned taking the pups on short rides in the boat to the shore for their routine bathroom breaks. Before this moment, I would swim on my back next to Ben while Max rode peacefully on my lifejacket. I know what you're thinking—what a little diva dog! Well, maybe a little. He floated across the lake with grace while I prayed to simply keep my head above the water and my muscles from cramping as I entered an uphill marathon with no blue ribbon at the end.

First, we had to get the kayak to the lake, and we had to do so without a trailer. As most of these stories go, there comes a point when the trip becomes less comfortable and more…difficult. This was that time. At some point on the trip, I had my body hanging out the window, trying to keep our shiny red treasure from taking flight. I'm still not quite sure why we didn't just buy the kayak at the lake.

We started the loading process, and somehow, it worked out that there was just enough room left in the vehicle for a Pomeranian and a Labrador. The kayak was tied to the top of the truck bed and protruded through the back window so I could "hold" it when necessary. It may sound a tad crazy, but you just never know with this Oklahoma wind, and we gambled everything on this magical Hulk-like grip I'd get in a moment of misfortunate catastrophe. Good thing all our eggs aren't always in one basket, and the winds that come sweeping down the plains have shown much mercy on some of our creative escapades. Luckily, I have yet to be forced into displaying my superhero-like abilities.

But we made it!

After a three-hour drive, we managed to haul the kayak down the dock to the boat slip and tie it securely. I was exhausted. At this point, I would not have minded if the shiny red kayak ended up in the depths of Grand Lake during the night. However, Devon was excited to fulfill his vision of the following morning while drinking coffee and exploring with the bravest navigator we know, Maxopher. It must be the same excitement Jesus experiences as we wake for the new day, anticipating how His children will use their purpose.

As it always seems to, morning arrived much earlier than I expected, and the two of them were off to discover hidden treasure. Trusty Ben stayed back with me. He's the life of the party, but not until after noon. Ben and I woke up late in the morning and headed to the ship store for treats, hoping to catch a glimpse of our sailors.

The moment I saw them, I fell in love with our shiny red kayak. It was like a picturesque scene from a movie made just for me: a handsome man sipping coffee with eyes that lit up like the morning sky. Then, there was

Max, his fur blowing in the wind, front paws up on the bow, scanning the water for pirates, mermaids, or maybe just his mom. It is one of the most peaceful snapshots in my memory.

Playing it cool, they gave us a sweet smile as they passed, and I waved from the dock as if I had seen the greatest captain of them all. Ben, of course, wagged his tail enthusiastically in approval.

That afternoon, we loaded the kayak on our boat and went out for a relaxing day on the water. To share in our excitement, our friends took turns piling into the kayak for a few individual joy rides. Now, it was my turn. I convinced the dogs to get in the mini vessel, and off we went to the shore. It was a little bumpy, but overall, smooth sailing. We all could have worked on our balance. Devon swam and nearly beat us to the shore, so in hindsight, the balance issue may have been more problematic than I recall.

We hung out in the shallow water while Ben ran around the shoreline, looking for anything he wasn't supposed to do. On the way back, we decided we should all ride on the kayak. Together is our favorite place to be, so it just made sense. Our friends waited at the boat in anticipation of one of the worst—yet most entertaining—ideas the Millers had ever had. Looking back, I can vaguely hear voices in the background reminding us of the weight limit, that we had a "horse" dog with us, and that the kayak technically only had one seat.

But we didn't care. We all piled into the kayak as if we were kids loading a ride at an amusement park.

Devon sat in the front and held Max. Max always secured VIP seating in every situation. Once they were settled, one hundred-pound Ben loaded up behind them. There wasn't any more square footage, so we did the only logical thing. We took the baggage compartment ropes off because that was the perfect place for me. Ol' Red's unsteadiness should have been a clue to stop, but we were too far into the plan to turn around now. I climbed onto the back and had time to take one breath, one sigh of relief. We all fit!

We were in—and then, we were out!

The kayak didn't just tip; it went from top to bottom in a quarter of a second. Every part of us was submerged in the water. I felt the sharp, rocky bottom of the cove and pushed back up. Ben was up, sneezing and blowing water out of his nose like a baby elephant at the bayou. Devon popped up, Max still in hand. Max had this talent for going from a handsome lad to a wet sewer rat, so you can imagine which one he was at that moment. He knew the difference, and he was *not* happy.

After making sure we were all accounted for, we began laughing out of embarrassment—or pure joy—or a little bit of both. I could see our friends' tears on the boat, amused at the spectacle we had made ourselves. At that moment, the cut on my foot, the poor look on Max's face, and the moss-filled, shiny red kayak were priceless.

We managed to get the kayak back to the boat and took a much-needed rest. I think most things that don't turn out as planned will turn out to be my better memories. Mary didn't plan to give birth in a stable. Paul didn't plan to spread the gospel through chained guards. Noah didn't plan to build an ark that would eventually save the world. But we still have rainbows, salvation, the mother of the King, and our Ol' Red. The purpose was never the planned destination; the purpose was protecting, sharing, and creating love.

In case you're wondering . . . Yes, we still have that kayak, and although it's not as shiny, it is filled with memories and the promise of our next big adventure. Never carrying more than its load capacity again, it has hauled Max and Ben to the shore many times. It has carried them to get ice cream with their mom and on the famous morning coffee trips with their dad. I believe the greatest wonder here is that they continue to ride with us. Without hesitation, they fearlessly jump in every time. They are eager to be with the ones they love, exploring the water like true skippers.

Dogs remind me of Jesus.

They would rather be with you in a kayak that may tip over than not be with you at all. I wish we could all be more like that, willing to start an adventure solely based on love.

Chapter 10

THE GOOD SHEPHERD

A shepherd takes care of the herd.

When I returned to work after maternity leave, I was thankful for my flexible schedule. I set up all my appointments around Devon's work schedule and my sister's college classes. They were on baby duty while I was out for several evenings a week. None of us had real baby experience, but we had dogs. How hard could it be? I was also grateful that Ben was there because he looked after everyone, always. Good shepherds take care of their flock, and Ben took pride in taking care of his family.

Let me back up a bit. Two years before the birth of my daughter, I fractured my leg. It's a good story, so I should probably pause to tell it. Devon and I had purchased some outdoor kitchen appliances. They came on a massive pallet, which was loaded into the back of Devon's truck.

A couple of friends had offered to help us unload it after work. In just a few hours, they would arrive, and we'd be grilling steaks in no time. Perfect!

Except we were impatient.

Devon and I crawled into the back of the truck, and with the pallet between us, we faced one another. I don't remember who spoke first, but the conversation led us to believe we could do this alone. "You are strong, Alex. If you lift with your legs, you'll be fine."

Max and Ben were both intrigued at this point and stared up at us with eyes of wonderment.

We pushed the pallet of kitchen appliances to the end of the truck bed. Each of us hopped off the truck and grabbed onto the pallet. We decided we didn't technically need to lift it, per se. We continued repeating, "All we have to do is guide it down." With each word, we felt more and more confident.

I took my stance, feet shoulder-width apart. "We can do this." I held onto the bottom of the pallet, fingers gripping the oak wood like I was Superwoman.

Deep breath. On three.

"We are just guiding it," we reiterated.

1 . . . 2 . . . 3 . . .

The pallet slid off the truck, and immediately, my upper body was pushed back, inevitably leaving my feet behind.

The pallet hit the ground. We had guided it—with my leg underneath it.

As I lay on the ground, Max and Ben remained loyally at my side. Just like the stories you hear of people moving cars during emergency situations, Devon picked up the pallet and freed my leg. The dogs were nearly on top of me. Devon called the emergency room to let them know we were on our way. He just needed to get the dogs in the house and me in the car.

Max and Ben wouldn't budge. Devon tried everything and, eventually, picked up Max to take him inside the house. During that time, Ben left, found a stick, and brought it to me, not in an attempt to play fetch but as a goodwill offering. He gently placed it at my side and slowly lay down with his head in my lap.

Ben's a good shepherd. He attends to his herd and doesn't leave the one for the ninety-nine. Finding your love language with God can shift your perspective in the most intense situations. I lay in the cool grass, injured, reflecting on God's presence through Ben's actions. Ben couldn't fix my leg, and he couldn't lift me into the car, but he served me where I was. He met me at my pain and offered peace in the unknown.

Now, fast forward a few years. I left for work (with my leg now completely healed) and left my two-month-old daughter with her dad, my sister, Max, and the good shepherd, Ben. Ben had been known to alert house guests in times of low blood sugar or distress, so he was a good back up sitter should the going ever get too tough.

Later that day, as I left work, Devon mentioned he was going to shower before meeting me for dinner. While Devon finished up some last-minute phone calls, my sister decided to sneak in a quick shower as well. The glass shower overlooked the bedroom, so she put my little one on the floor for some much needed tummy time. This worked out well since she wasn't crawling or mobile yet. With Ben lying beside her, my sister headed to the shower. She checked on my daughter often, and Ben lay snoozing beside her.

Taking advantage of the free time, Devon hopped in the shower next. Just like my sister, he checked on our daughter several times while she was preoccupied with her tummy time toys. He then headed to his closet to dress for the evening. A few seconds later, Ben came to greet him. Devon brushed it off as he was trying to hurry. Ben left and almost immediately returned. This time, he nudged Devon with his muzzle. Again, Devon asked Ben to go lie down. Ben left the room.

The third time, Ben returned with more urgency, as if he needed to go outside to use the bathroom. He would touch Devon with his nose and take a few steps toward the opening of the closet. Back and forth, back and forth. Devon got the hint and decided to walk Ben to the door and check on the baby. Ben beat him to her, kissing the top of her sweet head. Ben was trying to alert Devon that she had scooted—officially mobile! Although I don't know if I would call it a crawl yet, this was big time for us first-time parents.

While Devon had walked from the shower to the closet, our little one had decided to scoot for the first time. She had rolled off the play mat and was happily inspecting her "new" space. Thankfully, she was unharmed. Ben had been trying to alert Devon to the change in her surroundings.

Ben never gave up. He had paced back and forth between my daughter and Devon until he could get a reaction. After two failed attempts, Ben had proceeded to do the "potty dance" to get Devon to spring into action. Again, Ben was a faithful shepherd. He didn't leave the one. He didn't leave the lost. He found a way to comfort and protect.

My daughter was not injured that day. Honestly, she would have been fine until Devon reached her, but Ben knew something wasn't right, and he acted. It takes courage to act in spite of fear or uncertainty. I wish there were a class for this. I'd enroll but would still not be as faithful as Ben. It's a real gift.

Ben's a family-first kind of guy. He doesn't just love you when you're playing fetch. He isn't just excited to see you after your big promotion. He doesn't just flood you with dog kisses when you break world records. He loves you always. Anytime. Sitting in the sunshine, lying injured in the cool grass, or making sure you are safe after your first big scoot across the world, Ben is happy to be a good and faithful servant.

Dogs remind me of Jesus. They don't come for the righteous but for the broken.

He came for the sick, the injured, the lost, the struggling. He came for me and you.

Chapter 11

BE LIGHT

You find what you're looking for.

Recently, I had a conversation with one of the important women in my life who becomes nervous when she travels by plane. She prefers direct flights, and the thought of a layover often creates alarm throughout her nervous system. This is evident by the way she often calls me before a travel day and rapid-fires questions. "What time does it leave? How much time do I have between flights? What gate? How close is the bathroom? Where do I go when we deboard?" Despite the answers, she always follows with, "I'm never doing this again." (And then she does it again.)

This particular time we talked, she debriefed me on her last flight. She explained she had a layover, and when the first plane landed, she deboarded with the crowd. Then, she shared that she lost track of the next step and didn't know which gate to go to next.

When she realized she was lost, she looked around for help. I interrupted the conversation at this moment to remind her of the airline staff stationed at many of the gates, "They are there to help you."

She was quick to add that she would never ask a stranger for directions. Interested in her response, I asked, "Well, what did you do?"

She didn't miss a beat. "I just started scanning the airport for people with dogs. I like dogs and their people, and I trusted they'd be willing to help me."

Turns out, she was right. She showed her ticket to the first dog dad she saw, and two minutes later, she found her gate. I was struck by how clearly God was calling out to her. When I get flustered, I lose sight of the next step, too. Pausing can be good, but my pauses sometimes turn to panic, and the next thing I know, I'm circling Pluto when I was meant for Earth.

But in that instant, the message was clear. When you are lost, look for Jesus; he may be the guy with the traveling pup, the scent at your go-to coffee shop, or the view from the top of your favorite hiking trail. Just look for His answer. What you seek, you will find.

This conversation has become part of many thought-provoking reflections. I do most of my reflections on my morning walks. Fresh air is good for the soul, and I highly recommend it. I try to only think about *walking wonders* during this time. What's that, you ask? *Walking wonders* are ideas, dreams, and philosophies that don't fit into the day-to-day hustle. I like to give these things their designated space. On some of these walks, I'm not in a joyful mood. I'm not unhappy, but I am tired from the week's chaos, worried about something pea-sized that I've turned into a boulder, or sad about something I have no control over. Nevertheless, I give *walking wonders* their space.

Regardless of the mood, I always appreciate passing a dog. This is true for my youngest daughter as well. When she sees a dog on a walk, she yells, "I NEED TO PET YOUR DOG!" The word *need* here really makes me giggle because I feel the same way. It's a need, not a desire. I've noticed that if I see a dog on my morning walk, I smile. In return, the dog walker will, nine times out of ten, smile as well. It's contagious—joy. Perhaps it fades shortly after, but sparks of joy generate a ripple effect. For that split second, you and a complete stranger are blissful together, and it all started with a dog, a common reminder of light in the darkness.

Ben is my light in the darkness. My family recently went on a vacation, and Ben stayed home with a sitter. During the trip, Ben became sick. The sitter called, we made Ben a vet appointment, and I started researching early flights home.

Ben is aging, and the older he gets, the more he loves his mom. He doesn't dislike anyone; it's just that he has chosen not to listen to anyone but me. Even simple tasks like going outside or moving out of the walkway must be initiated by me, or it's a no-go for Ben. This is a small frustration for many people. (I secretly like it.) So, when Ben wasn't feeling well, and with his title of Momma's Boy, everyone was sure he just missed me.

I didn't hesitate while looking at my flight options because I instantly remembered the countless times Ben had met me at the door after a difficult day. I remembered the frequency of hugs, jumps, and tail wags I'd been greeted with in all my different seasons. Ben has no idea the day I've had or the state I'll be in when the door opens. No matter what, he's going to be waiting on the other side with the same enthusiasm. It really doesn't matter where you've been and what you've been through; Ben's love—and God's—are unconditional. So, I booked the flight.

While waiting for my departure the next day, I received a worrisome update. Ben was not eating or going outside without assistance. The sitter loaded him into the truck for his appointment, and the veterinarian had to carry him inside the office. After several scans and labs, Ben went home with a care plan and hopes that he would feel a little better the next day. Thankfully, that was the case.

I ended up staying on vacation one more day and flew home with the rest of my family. However, I was warned not to expect the same dog I had left, but to prepare for a more lethargic pup. When I unlocked the front door, take a guess where Ben was—right there to meet me. Tail wagging and ready for all the hugs. Everyone was surprised that, despite the circumstances and the last few days, Ben had preserved the energy to do what he does best—love his family. Even in the dark, he knew his light was coming home. I need to do that. I need to have faith so big it floods the storm. Imagine a life where we seek contentment in the commotion and joy in the gloom. What would that be like?

Dogs remind me of Jesus. They radiate light in the darkness. They pursue joy. Let's do that, too.

Chapter 12
MILLER ANNUAL KITE DAY

"Cherish the little moments." That's what we're always told. So, I often reflect on these little yet significant moments in my life.

Of course, this includes some of the common classics—the moment you were baptized, the birth of your children, the night you hugged a parent for the last time. Do you ever think of these? They often play in my mind in slow motion, and I ponder what I've been doing since then and if it's been as meaningful as it was fulfilling.

For me, it's important to try to keep these moments alive. I believe they make me a better version of myself. For example, in times of questioning my worth, I let my body return to that holy water that signified my devotion to be His.

When I'm overwhelmed, I think about how my daughter's namesake carried out her life with such grace despite her grief. When I need to feel love, I pay it forward. My dad was the best note writer: "Good Luck, Alex," and "I'm proud of you." These little notes filled my childhood backpack. They were always short, sweet, and to the point, but those notes are the highlight of my childhood reel when it plays in my mind. To continue his legacy, I write notes to my girls—short, sweet, and to the point: "You are brave" and "I'm proud of your kindness." I hope they feel the instant love that I so vividly remember, and I pray they will see the evolution of how a short, sweet message can change your life.

We are all familiar with the finales, the major moments that shape us, change us, and create strength. But what about all the others? What about the normal days that reach your core? How'd they get there? Why don't we talk about them more, all the stuff that happens in the middle of life? In English, "cross" is a synonym for "travel," and I wonder if that's a coincidence. I mean, it's the journey that makes the big moments bigger and the significant moments more memorable, right? Think about it. It's not just the birth of your child that makes your birth experience special. It's the months of anticipation. It's the loss in the trials. It's the yearning for a bigger purpose. These moments in the middle all culminate to bring you the joy that encompasses that day.

It's not the last memory with your parent that creates the grief. It's the countless high fives, the silent comfort of a protector's presence, or sometimes, the relationship that just never got to a peaceful place.

Unfold your finales.

I like to think that my memories are like the flight logs of Sky Turkey—our vintage Piper Warrior airplane. A flight log is the journal or diary of the day-to-day operations of an airplane. Big or small, the airplane's every milestone is recorded within its pages. What does your flight log say about you?

I scan my log (probably too much), but I've never been one to find comfort in the big moments. I live for the ordinary mess that creates those extraordinary finales. I love eating at home, listening to my children giggle with their friends, and sitting on the floor while petting my dog for no reason at all. I file these ordinary moments in a safe place because I know they are the foundation of God's best work.

More often than not, as I scan my internal flight log, I stop on a beautiful spring day in Oklahoma. I can still feel the warm grass on my bare feet and the sun warming my face, with the slightest bit of relief brought by the wind. It was an ordinary weekend after midterms in college, and I had just bought Max a kite. Now, you may think a kite is a waste for such a small creature, but that day with Max and the kite will go down in my log as one of the best of my life.

It had been over a year since learning of Max's physical limitations. While his small, five-pound size had previously been the only thing that kept him from keeping up with bigger dogs, his newly discovered physical limitations would keep him ground-bound for the rest of his life. Genetics played a role in his knee abnormalities, but the same leg was also slightly shorter than the others. Poor little guy!

Regardless, I was going to carry him around anyway, and now, we had an excuse. He could run and play, but jumping was not something that came easily. Max went on countless daily walks, and besides what I like to call his "gangsta lean," you'd never know he often struggled with mobility.

So, back to my kite day. Max was around two years old, and Devon and I packed dinner and the kite and headed to the park. It's important to note that when I hear "packed dinner and headed to the park," I picture some elaborate picnic with checkered napkins and a state-of-the-art charcuterie board. This was not the case. On the way out the door, we decided we were hungry and threw our favorite snacks in a plastic bag. Unfortunately, our taste buds have never been on the same wavelength. So, by the time everyone had their favorites gathered up, the bag was bursting at the seams.

Fancy doesn't follow us often, and luckily for us, fancy has never equaled fun.

Also, as you may have noticed, I tend to get overly excited about things, and Devon has learned to try to buffer any disappointment for me before it happens. For instance, when I started teaching Max tricks, he reminded me that Max wasn't a Labrador and might not eagerly embrace such learning.

But Max and I were on the same page. We ignored the haters, and he went on to learn impressive tricks such as rolling over, holding treats on his nose, and shaking my hand when I said, "Boomer Sooner." Living on campus in the Sooner State, you can imagine how popular that last trick became around our neighborhood. I can still see the countless smiles that simple and silly trick produced.

God has an effortless way of rewarding the power of work without going overboard.

So, for Max and me, the kite wasn't any different. I knew he'd love the kite because "better together" had become our new motto, and we were going to have a great time even if he just slept on the lawn. The greatest thing about our bond was that we didn't need some spectacular show. We were perfectly content just being together. Do you have friends like that?

It's remarkable how great adventures happen when you're truly content.

God's pretty clever like that.

So, kite time it was! We ate and assembled our sea turtle kite for takeoff. It had an expansive wingspan and streamers that fluttered in the summer wind, grazing the ground and making the grass follow in pursuit. We were blessed with perfect weather, and the kite took flight like a small toy Boeing. Without warning, Max was up and running. If the grassy lawn had been a pool of cool ocean water, Max would have given an Olympic swimmer the race of their life. I had never seen a dog with more might and pure joy.

He chased the kite's colored ribbons all afternoon with such bliss. The sight made me sit back in awe and wonder what he was thinking and imagining. What great adventure was he experiencing? Perhaps he was James Bond in the greatest car chase of his career. Or maybe he was Isaac Newton, firsthand experiencing the law of motion. Or was it a much simpler scene—just a dog with his family enjoying a day at the park? His innocent joy made me want to join in.

I hope to become more submerged in life's little moments, just like Max. Rarely do I believe we allow ourselves to be "all in," and I wonder, *what is holding us back?*

This day at the park, I was accidentally introduced to mindfulness. How had I lived so long without feeling the joy of being fully present? Why had it taken twenty-one years to belong so freely? At the time, I didn't realize that day was truly a golden moment for me, but as life went on, I would reflect back on this experience time and time again.

Then, years later, I decided to make it a holiday. That's right—I told you I love to get overly excited about things. This holiday is dubbed Miller Annual Kite Day, and it's celebrated every August 23. It's never been a big production, but it's purposeful, peaceful, and always fun. There is no food menu, fancy invitation, or designated time. It's a come-as-you-are event. Aren't those the best? If you're thirsty, bring a drink. Hungry? Grab a snack. If it's raining, dig out that old raincoat—or not. Bring a friend or two. The more, the merrier, because *life really is better together.*

We find some grass or sand and soar kites for hours. Regardless of the weather, the show must go on, so sometimes, you can find me running rapidly under the streamers, trying to make up for lost wind or damaged kite parts. By the way, why do kites have so many parts? Either I'm getting older, or these kites are becoming a little too intricate. Or maybe my kids just enjoy choosing these types of contraptions so they can watch me run around the yard like a crazy person. But those are all minor details. The truth is that I love every second of our beautiful kite days.

Miller Annual Kite Day is good for my soul.

It's so much more than a celebration. It's a reminder to brush off my flight log and enjoy the tour of life. I take this day and embrace my traveled miles. I celebrate all my mistakes, hard work, too-chaotic-to-breath days, and everything in between.

I hold the kite like a key as it unlocks my youthful freedom.

I like to envision the weight I carry on my shoulders being lifted by the kite. In the instant that the kite takes flight, my senses become more precise. The whole world just goes silent, and the only audible sounds are my daughters' giggles.

The only thing I see is little feet moving and jumping in excitement. Each smile is in slow motion, and every breath I feel to my core. In my hand, the handle of the kite feels like an extension of my body, and I let the wind carry my pain a little more than I should.

I close my eyes, but the dream doesn't go away. I'm living out my greatest prayer.

I'm present.

I'm free.

Why does it take a special day to have such a raw, meaningful experience? Why are these moments my favorite, yet I cave to the daily chaos of life? I'm still learning to live, love, and soar freely like the kite, but Max had it figured out years ago.

Dogs remind me of Jesus.

They bring peace to our present. We just have to open our hearts and let it in.

Chapter 13

ALL THE CHILDREN

I love dogs. So, it's no surprise that my children do, too. It must be genetic.

It may be familiarity. It may be that children learn from witnessing the habits and character of others. My habits itch with dog hair, and my character screams "Crazy Dog Lady" with no limits. There are never too many pups to love. But that's just me, unapologetically me.

Beyond raising the next generation of dog lovers, my wish is to protect my children while also encouraging them to dive into unwavering adventures. A few years ago, our church encouraged families to develop a family motto and live by the words daily. I loved this. We prayed:

"May Jesus be the foundation where our souls thrive on fearless adventure and loving others simultaneously."

I'll be honest. I have often failed in the pursuit of our family motto. My daughters have witnessed me cave to pressure and make unkind mistakes. They have watched fear overcome my faith and grief utterly consume my body for too long. But they have also observed that the life of an imperfect person can be revived with the love of Jesus despite her faults. That's the good part. That's the part I hope they never forget. That's honestly the part I need to remind myself not to forget.

We've all heard people say, "I work hard so my kids can have a better life," or "I stay late so my students can have more opportunities," or "I commit to my sobriety so I can watch my nieces/nephews grow up." But what about all of God's children? You're his child, too. What about doing these things for yourself?

This chapter is for the Children of God—for my girls, for me, and for you.

Zeus wasn't too old to learn new tricks, and we aren't too grown up to need the love of our Father. I want to challenge you to truly embrace this chapter and pause.

Reflect.

Go put your bare feet in warm grass.

Stop saving those shoes for a special occasion.

Turn up the music and really dance.

And rest without remorse.

It's our time to really give thanks for the goodness and purity of children and for the miracles of God perceived through the eyes of the innocent. These short stories are quick reminders that your heart holds your hope, and your God will always lead the way.

My oldest daughter was only two when her first dog succumbed to old age and walked so gracefully over the rainbow bridge. She had never known life without him, and I had never known a good life without him. I believe emotions are healthy, so I tried not to hide mine, and she soon learned that someone could grieve and be thankful at the same time.

She would ask me if I was sad. I was honest. I explained we can be sad about one thing while still being happy about a million others. She never saw the late-night showers of agony I endured, but she did see the grief. She saw real life. She saw tears of gratitude as we talked about him and pained tears when I often felt alone.

She has been blessed to see many doggie lifetimes. A year and a half after Max was gone, she was flipping through one of the many photo albums we had made of him throughout the years, and it just happened to be his birthday. As she was sifting through the pages, she shared little moments she remembered of him, either through her own experiences or from listening to others. It was beautiful. She had so many questions about birthdays in heaven: Did he celebrate his birthday? Was he older? Was there cake? Does the ice cream have sprinkles? How many friends came to his party? Was there a party?

Then, in the midst of all this, my three-year-old motioned for me to come closer, as if she were going to tell me the biggest surprise she'd ever kept. I was intrigued. I lowered my ear down to her little mouth and, through her smile, with strong conviction, she softly said, "And Mom, I bet Jesus is singing Happy Birthday."

Cue the tears. Without hesitation, I replied, "I know He is." Then I added, "And Max is really lucky because Jesus is a much better singer than Mom." The contagious giggles began, and I pray that if my memories ever fade, this will be one of my last.

My daughters are party planners. Again, it may be genetic or possibly due to familiarity. They have extravagant dance parties with fancy costumes, tea parties with every stuffed animal in the house, and elaborate concerts with guest performers. My oldest is always the emcee, and my youngest is always Jimmy Buffett. They make invitations, wrap "presents," and can find an infinite number of reasons to celebrate. We've literally had a "Happy Birthday" banner hanging in our house for five months straight, just in case they decide it's someone's special day.

The best thing about their parties is that everyone is invited, and each invitee is welcomed as the guest of honor. They often ask if Max is going to come to these parties. I try to explain his new role in our lives now, but they always have a way to get him there. "Mom, he can just borrow our Jeep."

I might have created two "loving monsters." Holidays are no different. For Christmas, we have the same conversations about stockings and why we only have ones for our immediate family. In their minds, anyone who has ever been to our house is worthy of a white knit stocking full of goodies. I mean, they make a good argument. Why are we selective? Does this come with age? When do we lose the will to include others? Maybe one day, I'll have a wall of stockings and treats for all. Someone should hold me to that.

The winter after the "birthdays in heaven conversation," the girls were going to bed on Christmas Eve. They counted the stockings one last time. (It's a thing. Perhaps an extra one will magically appear someday. More stockings, more fun?) As they crawled into their bunk beds, they asked, "Will Santa put something in Max's stocking, too?"

Clearly, "out of sight, out of mind" doesn't apply when the love has been abundantly faith-filled. Even toddlers know that.

So, of course, Max's stocking was full the next morning. It's magical how the miracle of Christmas can be remembered in a flash. It often takes a child to revive the lost child in you. Adult me collaborated with Santa to secure Max's goodies, and it was worth every single second because, as we hang the decorations year after year, someone always mentions the magic in Max's special stocking.

The feeling always comes when we are doing everyday tasks. "I miss him," they will say as we are eating dinner or driving down the street. Maybe they do really miss him. But sometimes I also think, *Well, maybe they just miss the me before he died*. Truthfully, at the beginning, I missed the *me* before he died. I grieved him, but I also grieved the me I felt for certain I had lost. I was more joyful and carefree with him here. At first, it took intentional effort to be blissful again. Our church did a series on consistency and creating healthy habits to change your life. It cultivated the idea that followers of Jesus aren't trying; we are training.

What a perspective!

I decided to read the Bible daily for a year. Within the first week, I witnessed a change in myself, but more importantly, in the girls I was raising. They started "reading" their Bibles and sitting with me while I was reading mine. They started asking questions and requesting that I share verses with them. You don't think they are watching, but they are. You don't think it matters, but it does. They love marking off the verses we've completed in my Bible, and I love witnessing their growth and love for Jesus.

My training isn't over. Yours isn't either.

I challenge us all to train more and try less, to be the foundation on which our families can thrive in the pursuit of fearless adventure and loving others simultaneously.

Dogs remind me of Jesus.

The more we love like them, the more others will, too. Our obedience today shapes our beautiful tomorrow.

Chapter 14

NOTE TO SELF

I am blessed. I am fortunate. I have food, shelter, and access to medical care. And for all of that, I am truly grateful.

This book, and specifically this chapter, is not a pity party or a woe-is-me moment. It is a moment of struggle, grace, and growth. A moment many others have experienced, yet for some reason, we are all hesitant to share. Why? Maybe for the fear of being judged? The fear of being misunderstood? The fear of appearing ungrateful?

The common constraint here is not the disapproval of our neighbors but the deception of a fear-based faith. So here I am, at the end of my story, sharing my deepest battles with my friends. May this chapter be a reminder that life is too blissful to be anything but raw, honest, and heartfelt.

I know my story isn't much different from many others. So, let me begin by setting the stage. I was a new mother. I wasn't healing as well as I'd anticipated. My baby cried frequently, and severe allergies would later be to blame. But at this point, I had no idea.

I had a two-year-old experiencing a cognitive leap beyond her years. She was reciting the months of the year and the pledge of allegiance and memorizing books, and I was feeling guilty that I couldn't give her more of my time. It was the height of the COVID-19 pandemic. We had just moved cross-country. We started a new business. My beloved Max was very sick. The list goes on, as it does for so many.

I was in daily contact with the veterinarian and knew the signs of ultimate struggle would soon present themselves.

It was a Thursday. I stayed up all night. Max did too. I gave him all my energy. He looked at me with pleading eyes, and my mind began replaying every time he'd saved me over the years.

Why couldn't I find a way to keep him here? I felt so lost and helpless, so I did the only thing I could think to do.

I spoke to God out loud. I wanted Max to hear my gratitude. I knew he could feel the love and comfort of the three of us holding each other: Max, his mama, and our God.

Grief changes you.

I've had the honor of grieving several very significant people and furry friends in my life. Yes, a true honor. Life is more fun with others, and I have been privileged with beautiful company over the years. I remember singing to my dad the morning he died. At the time, it felt like every happy childhood memory was a million miles away, but I was grateful to share his last moments.

When our closest family friend went to heaven unexpectedly in her twenties, I finally understood the phrase, "Life is too short," and the panic of not living each day to the fullest "knee deep in the water somewhere" truly set in. (Thank you, Zach Brown.)

When a neighbor who had grown to become one of our greatest mentors passed, it felt as if hundreds of our foundational blocks had crumbled beneath us.

But the day Max died was different.

Not in a measurable way. It didn't hurt more or less. However, my grief came from a different place. Max was the link that drew me to Jesus. My soul truly felt broken, as if I were losing my lifeline to grace, growth, and goodness.

Sometimes, life is too much all at once, most likely because I never do anything without thinking it through way too much. It's a curse. I don't write without fully preparing and analyzing each word. Until now.

This chapter is dedicated to the true depths of my soul.

The note you are about to read was written in the wee hours of the morning. I woke up on my own, which is rare with a newborn. Everyone was sleeping, and I awoke in a panic with an urge to cleanse my soul. The moment felt as if God tapped me on the shoulder and, when I glanced in His direction, He smiled.

We didn't need to say anything to be together. It was just Him and me.

God didn't tell me what to write that morning. Instead, I'd say He just held my hand. And isn't that the type of friend we all need?

Since that moment, I have craved this simplistic mental sensation. I try to plan for it (of course), and it never works. It reminds me of the moment my youngest daughter, who was only a one-year-old at the time, saw Cinderella for the first time in a restaurant at the top of the Disney castle. My daughter was wearing a Little Mermaid costume, Minnie Mouse shoes with the cutest tiny ruffle socks, and had her hair wrapped up high in a Queen Elsa bow. Mismatched and chaotic was a classic look for her.

When Cinderella stepped around the corner, I assumed my daughter would do the conventional toddler wave, but no. She got so excited, held out her dress, and started yelling "Look, look!" (pronounced "yook, yook"). She was so proud that Cinderella saw her just as she was. I think about the authenticity of that encounter, and it takes me back to that early morning I had with God.

The world was still, and I was begging heaven to "look, look." Here I am, mismatched and chaotic, praying God would see me, hear me, and set me free. I hope when I pass from this world, I don't enter heaven with a conventional wave. I plan to spread my wings wide and humbly say, "Look, look," for I am a Child of God—and so proud to be one.

So, here it is. A note from a tired momma to herself, who in the middle of her storm was grieving her lifeline to faith. But just when the last wave rolled off my back and I felt the pressing sand begin to sink under my feet, I looked up and felt the warmth of the Son.

Dear Me,

I've never felt more at home than when I was holding Max on my hip. And I'm already so can't-breathe, heart-wrenchingly homesick. A good friend reminded me that right after I got Max, we found out he had a hurt leg. At that time, I explained to my friend that we could return him, but I already loved him too much. Nothing describes my love for him more—it was instant and pure and the most unconditional love I've ever felt. He was my calm, my peace, my stay. He was the first time I remember God showing up extravagantly big in my life (hence why Max was "extra" most of his life).

For almost fourteen years, he was the physical presence of my spiritual journey. Now, the floodgates are open, and I've never felt such a drowning sensation.

Max was my daily reminder that God hadn't forgotten about me.

Wow, I think that statement alone is the truest thing I've ever admitted in my life . . . but God heals His people, and what if this was the plan all along? What if this is the silver lining? What if I just lived through the definition of faith—the belief that it's there without seeing, without hearing, and the enduring knowledge that the gift isn't carrying something on your hip but carrying it in your heart?

I may have been the one Max loved, but *we* are the ones God loves.

You are the one God loves.

Dogs remind me of Jesus. They're a constant reminder that God walks beside you, every day, every moment.

So, find your lure. Hold out your hand. And let God bless you, today and always.

AFTERWORD

For twenty years, I have always had a dog. My children have never known a life without Ben.

Until now.

Ben went to heaven, and I'm having a really hard time. At first, I didn't know if I should admit that. Not the former but the latter. I feel guilty. Guilty that I'm experiencing this much agony, again. Guilty because I know it could be worse, right? He's not a child or a parent. Grieving pets is complicated, which is ironic because their love was never filled with this uncertainty or hesitation. It's unlike any love you'll experience on earth. If you made it this far with me, you've either skipped to the back (don't do that) or love dogs just as much as I do. If that's the case, hear me out. Grieving with purpose is never wasted. It's never too much or unacceptable. Love that deep can't be sorted by a hierarchy, and you are not alone.

The week leading up to Ben's passing, I noticed a red bird every day on my morning walk. I had begun to rely on it. This red bird was like a hug from God, reassuring me that I would have a good day. We had a system, almost like a scheduled meeting, and I was loving the daily reassurance. The day Ben went to heaven, I didn't see the bird. That bothered me. I thought that I needed a sign from God that my faith was bigger than this pain. How were we going to make it without God saying, "Hey, Millers, I got you"?

Ben passed on a Friday, and by Tuesday, I had stopped thinking I would see the red bird. I went on my scheduled walk and slowly got ready for the day. As I did so, I searched for even a glimpse of hope that I would be well. Then, I remembered my daily scripture bracelet.

My good friend and colleague had gifted me a pastel-colored bracelet with a cross. I love it. It's subtly meaningful and over-the-top thoughtful. If you scan the NFC tag, it produces a daily scripture. That morning, I stared at the gift while I brushed my teeth. I decided I would wear the bracelet and scan it before heading to work. I was convinced the bible verse it presented would be insight into my day. This verse would get me through. *I needed it.* I brushed my teeth a little faster. I could hardly wait to see how my apprehension would be dismissed after reading a random NFC tag, labeled with a cross, that was surely a sign from God. *I'm a genius*, I thought.

I finished rinsing my toothbrush. I rustled to get the bracelet on. Perfect. But wait…

I couldn't find my phone. (At this point, I know you're not surprised.)

I began a hyper-focused search.

On the nightstand? No.

Under the couch? No.

In the fridge? (Don't ask.) No.

Phew, okay. Phone found.

Yes! I fumbled to connect it with the bracelet. Scan activated.

Nothing. Not one thing.

I'm serious. The site was down. Is that allowed with an NFC tag?

Believe it or not, I made it through the day, wearing the bracelet just in case it changed its mind.

Two days later, I had given up on experiencing a tell-all sign from God. Not because I didn't believe, but because I thought, *Well, maybe(ish) I don't really need it.* It was evening, and I was taking a few boxes to the trash. Trash pick-up day was the following day, so I had to walk to the street to reach the bins. I opened the lid, inserted the boxes, and looked up. There, at dusk, when I least expected it, was *my* red bird, just sitting, gazing at me.

I stared back. What seemed like years was only a few seconds. *Where have you been?* I ran back into the house, jumping, laughing, whispering to God that I knew he wouldn't leave me hanging.

Then, it hit me like a brick to the chest. I think I even put my hand on my heart. *God, I see what you did.* His plan is always bigger than our own. It's faith. Faith.

You don't look for faith—you live it.

Ben's life was always about faith. He was the last puppy of ten born several hours later than his littermates. His airway had to be cleared quickly to even give him a chance. He was Bad Ben for so long, but I always knew he'd be better.

Faith does that. It makes you better. It gave space for Ben to grow, and it gives space for us to grow, too. To grow in faith, in love, and in the capacity to hold joy. It's at the center of it all.

So, my friends, don't look for faith. It's time to put down this book and live it.

Here's to Better Ben, a better me, and a better you.

With love and in faith,

Alex

ACKNOWLEDGMENTS

Bryan, Alice, Olivia, Emily, and the MFS team: Saying thank you just doesn't feel like enough. With your skill and care, you took my vision to the next level—and made it even more beautiful than I imagined.

Kymmie: You brought my dream to life with your editing skills and patience. I have endless gratitude for your expertise and kindness.

Thank you to Brandy, Alex, and Kendra for proofreading, praying, encouraging, and believing in me.

To our former neighbors in Norman: You'll always be home, and I'll always have a porch swing—somehow, someway.

To the Bahama Clan and everyone who contributed to this journey: You are a consistent reminder that life is better together. Many of these stories are pure reflections of your grace and love.

A big thank you (and a side of giggling) to Aunt Granny Sav. You always see the best in Bad Ben . . . and in me.

Uncle Claud, the book's cover illustrator: I'm indebted to you. There are truly no words for your talent. Your selfless heart is, and forever will be, unmatched.

My girls: May this book serve as encouragement to always use your voice in the most faith-filled ways. Your presence is my greatest joy. I'm so proud of you.

Devon, thank you for inspiring me to share a piece of our love story with the world. In my mind, we'll always be just two kids in a Bronco, with Jimmy Buffett on repeat and dreams of raising good humans. And here we are . . . I'll never get used to this.

Zeus, Max, and Ben: This is for you.

And to you, the reader, and now my friend: Thank you for the company, and God bless.

In memory of my dad. Happy trails . . . and tails.

ABOUT THE AUTHOR

After years of writing as a passion, Alex has stepped into the calling of turning her love for storytelling into a ministry. With over twenty years of experience loving dogs and walking in faith, she weaves stories that inspire, uplift, and spread joy, always pointing to the goodness of God. As a licensed mental health therapist, Alex brings compassion and wisdom to both her clients and her writing, helping others find healing, hope, and purpose. When she's not creating, you can find her petting dogs or cheering on her favorite sports teams with her friends and family.